Going Live

Stay tuned...
the best
is yet to come!
Love,
Sally-Ann Roberts

Going Live

An Anchorwoman Reports Good News

SALLY-ANN ROBERTS

Photographs by
DON WESTBROOK

PELICAN PUBLISHING COMPANY
Gretna 1998

*The word "Pelican" and the depiction of a pelican are
trademarks of Pelican Publishing Company, Inc., and are
registered in the U.S. Patent and Trademark Office.*

Library of Congress Cataloging-in-Publication Data

Roberts, Sally-Ann.
    Going live: an anchorwoman reports good news / by Sally-Ann
Roberts ; photographs by Don Westbrook.
        p. cm.
    ISBN 1-56554-304-1 (hc. : alk. paper)
    1. Christian life. 2. Roberts, Sally-Ann. I. Title.
BV4501.2.R6417 1998
248.4—DC21   97-47661
                                                              CIP

Manufactured in the United States of America
Published by Pelican Publishing Company, Inc.
P.O. Box 3110, Gretna, Louisiana 70054-3110

I dedicate this book to my grandmothers,
Dorothy Henderson Roberts and Sally Suddeth Tolliver.
They exemplified the definition of the ideal woman
as described in the 31st chapter of Proverbs.

Her children arise and call her blessed;
her husband also, and he praises her:
"Many women do noble things, but you surpass them all."
Charm is deceptive, and beauty is fleeting;
but a woman who fears the Lord is to be praised.

Contents

Acknowledgments

I GIVE GOD, MY HEAVENLY FATHER, all honor, praise, and glory for the blessings of my life. I thank him for bringing loving lights into my life. Thank you, Lord, for giving me a dad like Col. Lawrence Edward Roberts.

Dad instilled in me a love for rocks. Years ago, Dad had a rock tumbler. He could take the most ordinary-looking rocks from the yard or gutter and transform them into beautiful polished gems. Sometimes, I feel as though I am in the rock tumbler of life. Even though I know I have a heavenly Father guiding the process of chipping away my rough edges, it still hurts. When I feel like fleeing the tumbler, I remember the lessons I will share with you in this book.

Thank you, Lord, for giving me a mother like Lucimarian Tolliver Roberts. She taught me, "If ifs and ands were pots and pans, there'd be no need for scrubbing." Mom, the eternal optimist, believes the best is always yet to come.

Thank you, Lord, for giving me a brother like Lawrence Edward Roberts II, whom I affectionately call Butch. Still waters run deep. Butch is quiet, but I have found during some of the lowest moments of my life that Butch has offered gentle wisdom. My big brother is a very good man.

Thank you, Lord, for giving me sisters like Dorothy Roberts McEwen and Robin Rene Roberts. They can make me laugh at my shortcomings and help me conquer them. Dorothy and Robin are my role models. My little sisters grew up to become my big sisters.

Thank you, Lord, for sending another sister into my life. Phyllis Nabonne has been my prayer partner since 1990, and what an inspiration she has been! We have made a commitment to walk in the spirit together until death do us part.

Thank you, Lord, for my mother-in-law, Ella Mae Craft. What a light she is in this world. You will read more about Ma Dear in this book. She is no fair-weather Christian.

Thank you, Lord, for sending into my life great friends like Cathy and Ray Harris and Karin and Noah Hopkins. They have, by their example, shown me how to be strong when faced with tremendous obstacles.

Thank you for sending Pattie Shoener at just the right time. It was Pattie who said, "Let's finish this manuscript now!" My three children scurried about while she transcribed the last chapter of this book as I read from my scribbled notes.

I am grateful to have a coanchor like Eric Paulsen. His unpredictable humor can be a refreshing breeze in the morning. There is nothing plastic about Eric. He is as real as they come.

I am grateful to have a colleague like Don Westbrook who so generously donated his magnificent nature photographs for this book. Don is perfection personified in his authoritative yet friendly presentation of the weather.

Thank you, Lord, for sending Angela Hill into my life. Her kindness sent my life into a new and exciting direction. She was and is truly God sent.

Thank you, Lord, for giving me sweet friends like Mrs. Lottie Mae Burnley, an elderly, Uptown New Orleans resident who knows no strangers. Over the years, I have learned much from Mama Burnley.

Thank you, Lord, for Gail Cauley Guidry. Gail is the newsroom administrative assistant at WWL-TV who helped me get this book off the ground.

Thank you, Lord, for my children, Judith, Kelly, and Jeremiah. I have learned much from them in my spiritual walk. If I, a frail human being, can love these kids as much as I do, how much more must our perfect Father love us all.

There are many, many people I should thank, and I will, Lord willing, in future books. But there is one person who cannot be put off until then. The number-one man in my life. My friend, my partner, my husband, Willie.

He believed in me before I believed in myself. This man was not born with a silver spoon in his mouth, but one made of stainless steel. He is a good man and my life-long partner. For his thirtieth birthday I gave him a plaque that reads:

> Willie, you mean the world to me
> In love with you I'll always be
> Life with you is oh so fine
> Lawn and housework you share down the line
> In good times and bad too
> Each day I thank God for you!

Thank you, Lord, for Willie. May God bless him.

May God bless you all.

Introduction

LIKE SO MANY PEOPLE in the Bible, Jeremiah, Moses, and Esther, to name a few, I felt, "Who am I to represent God?" I am not a minister. I don't have anything in my past that could serve as proof of any authority on the subject of spirituality.

Yet during a silent retreat at the Rosaryville Center in Ponchatoula, where this book was inspired, I was impressed by one great truth. There are no great people, only people who let a great God work through them.

I pray God will use this book to help someone. It is the account of one woman's spiritual walk. I have had my share of joys and disappointments in life, but I can truthfully say, through it all, God has been there.

God has been my rock through the storms. He is my strength.

Going Live

CHAPTER 1

Life Is Live

There are no tape delays,
or instant replays.
You've got to live and give it
all you've got.
You've got to care and bear
a whole lot,
because life is live!

THAT'S PART OF THE RAP I share with young people when I am asked to speak to them about making the most out of their lives. I usually give them a three-D formula for success.

> **Decision:** Write down specific goals. Where do you want
> to be in 5-15 years?
> **Discipline:** Do the work required. How much do you
> want success?
> **Divinity:** Study and pray everyday. Who is guiding your life?

But to effectively implement the three-D formula for success, you've got to realize the importance of time. This is true whether you are seventeen or seventy. Our actions or inactions ... words or silence ... can have major consequences both good and bad, because life is live.

I work in an industry that places a premium on being live. When I first started working in television news in the mid-1970s, live shots were rarely used. It took a major effort and a major story to pull those off. Now if the mayor sneezes at five, six, or ten we are there to bring you live coverage. If he gets an attack of the hiccups, we'll break into programming.

Our technology has moved faster than mere human beings can keep pace. I remember the Cabildo fire in 1988. My afternoon work was winding down, and I was looking forward to heading home. Suddenly across the fire scanner came word of a one-alarm fire. One-alarm fires do not usually cause a ripple in the newsroom, but word of a one-alarm fire at the Cabildo, one of the most historic buildings in the city, caused a tidal wave of activity. I was immediately sent to the scene. A live truck maneuvered as quickly as possible down the narrow French Quarter streets.

It took us only a few minutes to get to the scene since WWL-TV is located on the edge of the French Quarter. But by the time we arrived, the Cabildo, the place where the Louisiana Purchase was signed, the place that held such valuable artifacts as Napoleon's death mask, was engulfed by flames.

I had hardly gotten my bearings. I had only been on the scene about fifteen minutes when chief engineer Dennis Giurintano handed me a microphone, saying the station was ready to break into programming with a live shot. And with that, photographer Bob Eutsler focused the camera, and we were on the air live.

My palms still sweat when I think of that day. Thank God for the museum director, Jim Sefcik, who was there immediately to provide information on camera. That is seat-of-your-pants journalism. That is television news.

That is life. Live from New York, New Orleans, or Wichita, this is your life. There is no stopping the tape for an edit job, no fast forwarding past the boring or painful stuff. Lord knows there have been many times I wished I could rewind events as easily as videotape.

One of those times was back in September of 1981. I was sitting in an edit booth looking at a videotape of a football play. Sixteen-year-old Tim Harry was the pride of his town of South Vacherie, Louisiana. Many at St. James High School considered the six-foot-two-inch star athlete a big brother. There seemed to be nothing in which Tim did not excel . . . baseball, basketball, track. And in his senior year, he decided to add football to his list of accomplishments.

But in the last three minutes of the third quarter of the Wild-cats' game against West St. John High, Tim made the last tackle of his life. On the tape I saw a strong, healthy young man sprinting across the field, the future ahead of him. Then bodies collided. Everyone got up except Tim. He lay on the field unable to move.

Even as Tim lay on the ground paralyzed, he managed the strength to reassure his worried family that he would be okay. A helicopter with paramedics arrived and quickly carried Tim to the hospital.

Two days later Tim Harry died of a fractured neck. The screen went black as the tape ended.

I rewound the tape and watched as the helicopter reap-peared. The paramedics took Tim back to the field. I watched as the rewinding tape showed Tim getting up from the ground and running backward down the field from where he began his trek.

We can't rewind life. Every moment is precious. Every moment we spend with our loved ones should be cherished. Tim Harry died on September 8, 1981. When I spoke to Tim's mother, Marie Elizabeth Harry, fourteen years later, she told me she was in the process of cooking red beans and rice. She said she had just been chuckling to herself at the memory of Tim's walking into the house and being overjoyed to find a pot of red beans on the stove. It was his favorite dish. Now when-ever she prepares it, Mrs. Harry says she can smile, knowing that she and her son shared the simple joys of life while they could.

As we are planning our careers and personal goals, we should not lose sight of the wonder of life. Put your finger to your pulse and as you feel the rhythmic beat, thank God for one more chance to love, to share, to be.

Dear Lord,

Please help me to use each moment of every day wisely. Keep me from wasting the precious gift of time.

Through Jesus Christ I pray. Amen.

LIFE LESSON #1
Don't Waste Your Time

While I was contemplating the message I wanted to convey in this lesson, my thoughts were rudely interrupted by the alarm clock. The sharp constant ring must have been sent by God, because it caused me to remember that each of us has an alarm clock. One day the alarm will sound and our time here will be up. We will arise to a new life.

We have a finite time on this earth. Only God knows how much sand we have left in the hourglass. We cannot afford to waste this precious time. This is what I have done to make the most of the time I have.

1. *Pray.* I asked God why he gave me life. He gave each of us gifts and talents to enrich his kingdom on earth. We certainly were not placed on earth simply to enrich ourselves. I have never seen a suitcase strapped to the top of a hearse.

2. *Write a mission statement.* My friend Cathy Harris taught me that. A mission statement answers the question, "Why am I here?" Cathy says she knows God placed her here to support children. My mission is to be an encourager. What's yours?

3. *Set priorities.* My priorities are simple: God first, family second, friends third, and everything else behind those three. I cannot be all things to all people.

4. *Use the mission statement and listed priorities to develop a schedule.* My schedule, for instance, calls for me to visit a school every Tuesday afternoon during the school year. And I am available for speaking engagements that fit my mission every other weekend. I feel called to speak but that is only part of my mission of encouragement. My schedule gives me plenty of time to fulfill other parts of my mission such as supporting my family and friends.

5. *Take time out daily for quiet time with God.* This is the most important thing I do each day, and I will share that in detail in Life Lesson #3.

6. *Enjoy life's blessings.* I've always wanted a house on a lake or by the ocean. Recently it dawned upon me that I lived on a body of water for more than thirteen years and never appreciated it. So what if it was a drainage canal? It was a peaceful body of water that often attracted ducks and reflections of the sun. Whatever I have...wherever I am...I will enjoy my life. Paul said it best in Phil. 4:11-12:

> I have learned to be content whatever the circumstances. I know what it is to be in need and I know what it is to have plenty. I have learned the secret of being content in any and every situation, whether well fed or hungry, whether living in plenty or in want.

7. *I have taken as my personal motto, "Only what I do for Christ will last."* When I am at death's gate I will not be thinking about who liked or didn't like me. . . or houses...or cars...or jewelry. I will not care how much money I had in the bank or whether I was on the "A" social registry. I will not be thinking about a network anchorship or a syndicated television talk show. The only thing that will matter to me at that time is the only thing that should matter to me now: God's approval. This life is only a blink of the eye in the space of eternity. I pray I will hear my Lord say, "Well done, my good and faithful servant, well done." The teeth-gnashingly painful alternative is to hear him say, "I never knew you."

Dear God,
  Show me what You would have me do. Please, Lord, forgive me for

those times I have given in to human concerns at the expense of spiritual matters. Lord, I want to be pleasing in Your sight.

Through Jesus Christ I pray. Amen.

CHAPTER 2

Getting a Peace of the Rock

A Storm Approaches

BACK IN 1981, my husband, Willie, and I went to bed on Sunday night after a warm dinner with my parents. But I was not at peace. A new anchorship had opened up at Channel 4 and I wanted it. I wanted this position so badly I was consumed by it. I prayed for the job. I had been a reporter at New Orleans' CBS affiliate WWL-TV for several years, and I felt I was ready to graduate from the city hall beat to the anchor desk.

My mind was consumed that Sunday night with thoughts of dread and hope. What if I didn't get the promotion? What if I did? Could I handle getting the job? Could I handle not getting the job? Finally, I was able to drift off to sleep. Then the telephone rang.

Willie reached for the receiver and groggily said hello. Immediately he bolted upright and turned on the light. The conversation was short, but it changed Willie's and my life forever.

After Willie hung up the phone, he quickly grabbed his pants while explaining to me that Richard, his brother, had been in an automobile accident, and it didn't look good. We both experienced a trauma we had never known before. I uttered a frantic prayer. It went something like this: "Please, Lord, don't let Richard die!"

That night is a blur. I remember speeding out of New Orleans. As Willie drove with eyes wide with worry and anxiety, I prayed silently to God that this was some awful mistake. We were told Richard had been flown by helicopter from Hattiesburg Memorial Hospital to the trauma unit in Jackson, Mississippi. That was where his best chance of survival could be found.

When we got to Hattiesburg, Mississippi, the police pulled Willie over for speeding. Willie told the officer that he was trying to get to his brother. Hattiesburg is a small town, and the officer knew about the accident. He compassionately let Willie go without a ticket, only with a request that he slow down. Willie tried to get some more information from the officer about the accident, hoping that the officer would say that Richard's injuries were not as severe as we had been led to believe. But he confirmed our worst fears when he hesitantly said we should waste no time getting to Jackson.

When we got into Jackson, the street lights passed like a surreal blur of white. I felt as if we had entered the twilight zone. The thoughts that had occupied my mind the day before seemed laughably trivial. I could not have cared less now about who got the anchorship. Just please, Lord, let Richard live.

Willie and I found Ma Dear in the waiting room of the trauma unit. She embraced us, and with controlled calm told us that Richard had just come out of surgery. He was alive. There was hope that he would pull out of this, but it didn't look good.

I went to the hospital chapel to pray as Willie waited for permission to see Richard. I found the large Bible on a kneeling stand opened to the 37th Psalm: "Be still before the Lord and wait patiently for Him."

I knelt where so many anguished souls had knelt before and wept. My tears fell onto the Bible verses as I spilled out my heart to God. I pleaded, as I never had before in my life, for a miracle.

After awhile, Willie came into the chapel and tried to tell me how Richard looked to him. He was trying to describe Richard's injuries. Then he suddenly stopped, unable to go on, and did something I had never seen before. He burst into tears. He cried, gasping for breath like a child. I held Willie in my arms and prayed even more resolutely for a miracle.

In the Storm

During the weeks that followed, I fasted and prayed. Spiritual brothers and sisters came to Richard's bedside to pray. Ma Dear seldom left her son's side. Wiping his brow . . . talking to him . . . holding his hand . . . Ma Dear's love for Richard knew no bounds. All the time Richard remained in a deep coma. My perspective of life changed.

I was surrounded in that hospital by misery. Every day new people were wheeled in. The weekends were especially bad. So many automobile accident victims were brought in that I felt as though I were in a war zone. The relatives came into the waiting room late at night, dazed by a phone call similar to the one that had awakened Willie and me what seemed like eons ago. Willie, Ma Dear, and I became veterans of grief. We had heard it all before.

I will never forget an elegantly dressed couple who came into the waiting room. The woman was wearing a glittering evening gown and had a mink stole. She and her husband had received news of their son's accident when they returned home from a social event. The woman with hair beautifully styled and face flawlessly made up had just entered the twilight zone. Her son, we were later told, would never walk again.

Outside the hospital life seemed unreal. I saw people laughing and wondered what they found so funny. How could they enjoy eating and going to the movies? Our life for the weeks in Jackson was one of going from our hotel room to the hospital. Later Ma Dear was able to find lodging at a rooming house that the good folks of Jackson had set up for family members who needed a place to stay while their loved ones were in the hospital. The churches took turns providing free meals. There is an old saying: "I walked a mile with happiness and she chattered all the way. . . . I walked a mile with sadness and ne'er a word did she say; but, oh, the things I learned that day."

We learned a lot about compassion, in our walk with grief. Nurses gave more than the job description required, and the rooming house volunteers treated strangers like sisters and brothers.

Oh, the Things I Learned That Day

I learned a lot that day from strangers. I remember one woman in the hospital waiting room whom I did not like. She was cheerful . . . too cheerful. Didn't she know we were worried? Richard was in a coma that we were told he might never come out of. And here was Mary Poppins talking cheerfully on the telephone and with a ready smile for anyone in her vicinity. I thought angrily to myself, *just because her son is doing well is no reason for her to take our grief lightly.*

Then I found out her son was not doing well. Her son had been in and out of the hospital many times in his young life, and this was to be the last time. Her son was dying and she had only one decision left to make: whether to let her son die in the hospital or at home. I felt ashamed of myself. I had judged this woman in my heart as being an unfeeling, shallow person when in actuality she was a saint. Oh, the things I learned that day about courage and faith.

I was to learn more as the weeks and months passed. Richard was transferred from Jackson to the hospital in Hattiesburg and then to a nursing home. He never came out of the coma. Then one day our phone rang again.

Ma Dear told Willie he should come to Hattiesburg to visit Richard. Willie said there was no need for me to come. He didn't think it was serious. Richard had been through numerous setbacks before and had pulled through them. Shortly after Willie left, the phone rang again. Richard was dying.

I drove to Hattiesburg. By the time I reached the hospital, Richard was dead.

Willie and Ma Dear were by his side when Richard, at the age of twenty-one, took his last breath. Willie continued talking to Richard after he died. Willie felt that his spirit was still in the room, and he told Richard that he and Ma Dear would be fine and that he should follow the light. He told Richard not to feel bad about leaving them, that they would meet again someday.

I cried again for Richard as I had done so many times during the four months he lingered in a coma. Yet Ma Dear was strangely at peace. As we left the hospital, I offered to drive and she said she could drive. Ma Dear said she always worried about Richard but she said she would no longer have to worry about him because he was now safe. There was no bitterness that the God we had prayed to all of these months had not granted us the miracle of healing we had begged for. In God's infinite wisdom he gave Ma Dear another kind of miracle . . . the peace that passeth all understanding.

The automobile accident was not the first time Richard had been in a life-threatening situation. As a baby, Richard had contracted pneumonia, and the doctors had warned Ma Dear that he might not live. But God answered prayers and Richard survived. Richard stayed with Ma Dear for twenty-one years . . . giving her joy and love.

Why?

Richard was a good child who loved his mother and enjoyed spending time with her. He went to church on Sunday without being prompted. He took great care in choosing her Christmas, birthday, and Mother's Day gifts. The two of them watched television together. They especially liked professional wrestling. They would roar with laughter at the antics of Cowboy Bob Kelly or Gorgeous George. Kind, gentle Richard had been called home.

As I drove to work one day after the funeral, I was filled with questions. As I passed pedestrians on the street, I pondered, "Why Richard?" Why did Richard die when there are so many people who are selling and abusing drugs, so many people who kill and hurt others, yet they are alive today and Richard is dead? It didn't seem fair. I'd asked that question years before when Cindy Wilson, my former co-worker at WDAM, was tragically killed in an automobile accident. She left behind a young child, a devoted husband, and a community that loved her. Why was Cindy called home so early? I would ask that question again many times over the years.

Why did little Jenny, the child my prayer partner, Phyllis, and I prayed for, have to die of cancer at the age of seven? We sat at the funeral and watched as her little classmates in school uniforms filed past her coffin.

Why did my friend Ella Louise Ifford's son Mark have to die? He was shot to death in broad daylight by a deranged gunman. Why was Norman Shepard, the director of the Gospel Soul Children, murdered as he returned home from choir rehearsal? The night of his wake people young and old sobbed in the crowded church. Many more who could not get inside wept on the sidewalk.

Why were my good friends Geraldine and Willie Jordan forced to say good-bye to two sons in two years? Kevin and Willie Jr. were loved by so many people.

And then there was Gregory. One night as I was hard at work on a speech for the Minority Male Consortium about saving the children, the phone rang.

My husband handed me the phone over my objections, saying, "I think it's important." It was Adrine, my friend Cathy Harris's sister, calling with the bad news. Cathy's son Gregory was dead. He had been shot to death in his home.

Again, another no-suspects, no-motive disaster had struck. This time the victim's mother was my sister, my girlfriend, Cathy. Cathy who, with me, founded Each One Save One. I drove over to Cathy's house, feeling as though I were once again in the twilight zone. Cathy had dedicated her life to saving children, and now her son had been taken away.

As a television reporter, I have seen so many tragedies. Children killed in house fires . . . wives killed by estranged boyfriends and husbands . . . families dying of carbon monoxide poisoning because of a faulty furnace . . . automobile accidents . . . plane crashes . . . diseases . . . every day there is a new tragedy to report. One day I unburdened my concerns to my mother, and she pulled a pad out of her purse and began to write the words to an old hymn she used to sing as a child. I keep that piece of paper tacked to the wall in front of my typewriter. It says:

> *Farther along we'll know more about it*
> *Farther along we'll understand why.*
> *Cheer up my brother and live in the sunshine*
> *We'll understand it all by and by.*

What Was Meant for Evil . . .

Ella Louise Ifford has become a source of comfort for many other grieving mothers. They are drawn to her because they know she feels their pain.

Noman Shepard's legacy lives on not only in his family but in a student Bible study group organized at a local high school by students who were inspired by his life.

Willie Jr. and Kevin Jordan had been sick all of their earthly lives. Although Geraldine, Willie, and their beautiful daughter, Akiia, greatly miss them, they take comfort in knowing that the bodies Willie Jr. and Kevin now enjoy have been raised imperishable, in glory, in power . . . a spiritual body as revealed to us by Paul in I Cor. 15:42-44. The Jordans' faith has given strength to many.

And as for Cathy, the tragedy that could have derailed her

emboldened her instead. She became more determined than ever to reach out to the children. She said that if someone had been able to reach her son's killer as a child, her son would still be alive.

Ma Dear's house that had been empty is now full again with the laughter of children. At this writing, Ma Dear is raising three wonderful foster children. "What happiness is there for you who weep, for the time will come when you shall laugh with joy"—Luke 6:21.

A suburban newspaper carried a poem I wish I had clipped out and kept. The poem compared this life to being on the underside of a quilt. As we look up we see lines going every which way for no apparent reason. But when we leave this life we will get to the other side and be able to see the top of the quilt. We at last will be able to see the design of our life. We will understand that what appeared to be haphazard workmanship was really the craftsmanship of the Master.

The Bible tells us that Joseph was sold into slavery by his brothers. Yet he rose from slavery to become ruler of Egypt, and ultimately saved his family from starvation. Joseph had every reason to be bitter over the treatment he had received at the hands of his brothers. Yet Joseph said to his brothers in Gen. 50:20, "As far as I am concerned, God turned into good what you meant for evil, for He brought me to this high position I have today so that I could save the lives of many people."

Lord,

Please help me to use the storms of life to glorify You. Open my eyes to Your lessons so that I will be strengthened by life's challenges, not weakened.

Through Jesus Christ I pray. Amen.

LIFE LESSON #2
Going On

Writing a life lesson on death is therapeutic for me, because just this day I attended the funeral of four-year-old Kirk White and his nine-year-old sister, Brittany. They were killed when the car they were riding in crashed into a lagoon. Their mother, Tanya, swerved to miss a dog and her car flipped over into the water. Despite her frantic efforts and those of nearby Southern University students, the two children perished.

Tanya and her husband, Kirk, came by my house a couple of days after the accident. Kirk's mother lives down the street from me. I prayed before going into the living room to comfort them. What in the world could I say to them? Wouldn't talking about God's love, after they had just lost two children, be as cruel as pouring salt into a gaping wound?

When I walked into the living room I found the two wounded souls, yet they exuded a strong faith. They said they didn't understand why their children had been called home so early, but they did not question God. Kirk said he was glad that his wife's life was spared. They both said that it would be hard to go on without little Kirk and Brittany, but they trusted God to give them the strength they needed.

Kirk and Tanya will go through the stages of grief. That is human. But they will also know peace. That is divine.

Little Kirk went to the same preschool that my son attends. The little preschoolers in Kirk's class miss their friend who loved music and playing in the water. Four-year-old Emma had a hard time dealing with Kirk's permanent absence from school. But one day she told her mother that she had figured it out. She said, "Kirk is in heaven. Jesus is in heaven. Jesus is alive. So Kirk is alive too."

That is the bottom line of this lesson. We must have the faith of a child. We know, as the old saying goes, we are either in a storm, just coming out of a storm, or headed for a storm. The only way to survive the storms of life is to cling to the Rock.

> *On Christ the solid Rock I stand.*
> *All other ground is sinking sand.*
> *All other ground is sinking sand.*

Lord,
> *Have mercy on Your children.*
> *Through Jesus Christ I pray. Amen.*

CHAPTER 3

Grandmother Sally's Gift

WHEN MY GRANDMOTHER SALLY WAS VERY ILL, I flew to Akron, Ohio, to be with her. She was attached to a breathing tube and could not talk. She beckoned for a pad and she wrote, "I am ready to go home." She then pointed upward. Grandmother Sally had lived almost ninety-two years. She had seen great triumphs and tragedies. Her husband was an alcoholic but she lived to see him join Alcoholics Anonymous. She watched one of her babies die of whooping cough and three others grow into successful, kind adults. She lived through the depression and two world wars . . . and she lived through the days of segregation and integration.

Grandmother Sally gave us many gifts in life but perhaps the most precious gift was given to us after she died. As we were looking through Grandmother's apartment after she died, we found journals everywhere. Grandmother kept a daily journal on everything from large notebooks to scraps of paper. The daily entries were brief. Most were only two or three lines long. One entry was repeated over and over again through the days, months, and years of her journals. "I had quiet time today."

I asked my mother what Grandmother was talking about. "What is quiet time?" Mom told me it was the time of day or night Grandmother sat and meditated. Grandmother believed not only in talking to God but also in listening to Him. She dedicated a portion of each day to studying God's Word, praying, and then waiting patiently in silence for God to speak to her heart.

After my mother explained the meaning of quiet time, I remembered walking in my grandmother's living room one day and seeing her sitting on the sofa with her eyes closed and the curtains drawn. I know now that Grandmother was not sitting alone in that room. And I know that I am not alone either.

I had a strange spiritual awakening about a year before Grandmother died. At least I thought it was strange. But in looking through Grandmother Sally's journals I learned my daily conversations with God were a continuation of a family tradition. And I had a name for it because of Grandmother... Quiet Time.

In March of 1991, I came home down in the dumps. I was informed that the early edition news program I anchored was being canceled as a cost-cutting move. I was devastated. I desperately wanted someone to talk to but no one was available. I was alone. Then a thought occurred to me. Why not talk to God?

Up to this point in my life, my prayers were pretty much a list of requests combined with the Lord's Prayer. I had never thought of trying to converse with God. I had heard people say, "I got this Word from the Lord." But I always thought that was just a figure of speech. After all, how would God communicate with us? *This is God!!!* Nah.

But anyway I was at my wit's end. So I sat down and wrote a letter to God. It was to be the first of many. One of those early letters that I was able to find paints the picture of gloom that encompassed me:

I go to bed tonight frustrated with my life. I can't seem to get anything together. I have lost the Early Edition and people are being laid off at the station. Willie's company is in an embryonic stage. He is depending on me keeping my job. My stock at the station is falling fast, both figuratively and in real terms. I fast and pray, yet it seems no answer comes.

After writing my letter to God, I was quiet. Before I knew it I was writing thoughts that flowed into my mind . . . soothing thoughts that I know must have come from God.

March 25, 1991:

You are not drifting. You are on a course I have directed . . . I love you, Child. I will not bring you into situations I have not preordained as beneficial for your ultimate good. I am with you, piloting your course. There are many things happening now that are frustrating you, but they are only preparing you for a mighty miracle.

And many wonderful things did begin happening in rapid succession. My "Dear God" letter of April 23, 1991, was one of unbelievable thanksgiving:

So much is happening in my life right now. I was just told last week that I will anchor the weekend news. . . . I have also been told I will anchor the 10 P.M. show. . . . I know this achievement and newfound opportunity are gifts from God. It is nothing short of a miracle!

Since March 1991, I have enjoyed a daily supply of soul food. I get up very early in the morning, not just because I have to now as coanchor of the "Eyewitness Morning News," but because it is the quietest time of the day. The family is asleep and I can be still. I know the true meaning of the hymn

I come to the garden alone
While the dew is still on the roses.
And the voice I hear falling on my ear
The son of God discloses.
And He walks with me, and He talks with me,
And He tells me I am His own;
And the joy we share as we tarry there,
None other has ever known.

Merciful Father,

I want to walk with You. Speak to my heart. Guide my footsteps so that I will not run ahead of You nor lag behind. Lord, I yearn to walk with You. Please show me how.

Through Jesus Christ I pray. Amen.

LIFE LESSON #3
"Hush, Somebody's Calling Your Name"

If you are too busy to be alone with the Lord, you are too busy. Food gives your body the sustenance it needs. But the soul food that you devour during quiet time can give you supernatural strength. "I can do all things through Christ who strengtheneth me." (Phil. 4:13 KJV)

Make time to tap into your divine energy source. And more Americans are doing just that. According to a 1997 survey conducted by the Pew Research Center, 53 percent of those polled said prayer is important to their daily lives. Ten years ago only 41 percent said prayer is important.

Your quiet time may come late at night, or you may have to set your alarm clock and get up an hour earlier each day. I prefer morning quiet times because I need a boost to start my day. You on the other hand may prefer night quiet times to settle down after a hectic day and focus on the lessons learned. Do whatever works best for you.

The Elements of Quiet Time. SSSHHH!

1. Silence. Choose a time of day when you can be alone with no distractions. Set aside a definite hour for your quiet time, and make a commitment to stick to your daily schedule of prayer and meditation. Very soon it will become a pleasant habit you look forward to each day.

2. Situate. Choose a place in your home to be your prayer place. It could be a walk-in closet, your kitchen table, the living room, or the den. Whatever place you choose, go to the same place every day. Make that space your place of prayer.

3. Study. The purpose of quiet time is to get to know God and His plan for your life. We can't know God if we are not

regularly reading His Word. People have different ways of reading the Bible. Some people start in Genesis and read a chapter or two a day until they get through Revelation. Pres. Jimmy Carter and his wife read aloud from the Bible in this manner. Once they get through Revelation, they start all over again at Genesis. I study the Bible by opening it, after prayer, to a passage at random. I am constantly amazed by the way God leads me daily to the perfect Scripture for me.

Find the Bible that is right for you. There are many different versions. I prefer the *Life Application Living Bible.* Many people prefer the King James or New Revised Standard versions.

I also enjoy reading a daily devotional each day. *The Daily Word, Streams in the Desert,* and *Acts of Faith* are some of my favorite devotionals. I also read Susan Taylor's *Lessons in Living* and Dr. Norman Vincent Peale's *Positive Imaging* on a regular basis.

There are many books that will feed our spirit. The most important one is the Holy Bible. Read and learn. Read and find guidance.

4. Honor. Give God the glory He deserves. We are before the throne of the great I Am! Praise Him and glorify His name as the Spirit leads in prayer, song, or recitation of Bible verses.

5. Humble. Humbly seek God's face. We can bring all of our cares to Him. We do not have all the answers, but He does. Speak to God as you would to a loving father. Lay out your concerns. We do not need to clean ourselves up to go to Jesus. He accepts us just as we are.

6. Heed. After you have poured out your concerns to God, be quiet and listen to that small inner voice. God speaks to us through our thoughts.

The Bible says, "Finally, brothers, whatever is true, whatever is noble, whatever is right, whatever is pure, whatever is lovely, whatever is admirable—if anything is excellent or praisewor-thy—think about such things" (Phil. 4:8 NIV). When God is speaking, the thoughts will be positive, peaceful, and provi-dential. God is not the author of confusion. He is faithful to respond to us when we call Him. But be careful not to confuse good with evil.

Just as God speaks to us through our thoughts, so does the devil. Never underestimate the craftiness of the great deceiver. He knows the Word and will try to use it as he did in trying to entice Jesus in the desert where Jesus was fasting for forty days and nights. One test of knowing whether the thoughts are of God is to compare them to His Scripture.

God would never encourage us to do anything that goes against His commands. For instance, if a husband is tempted to have an extramarital affair, God would never say that's okay. He's not going to say, "Yeah, man, do what comes naturally." God is not a god of convenience who bends to our whims.

To learn more about how to know God's voice, read the Reverend Charles Stanley's excellent book *How to Listen to God.* That is the last gift Grandmother Sally gave to me.

I was visiting my grandmother's apartment while she was in the hospital and noticed the Reverend Dr. Stanley's book on her coffee table. Inside she had underlined passages that she particularly enjoyed and scribbled notes in the margins of several pages. When I went to the hospital to see Grandmother as I was leaving Akron, Ohio, I asked if I could borrow her book. She was on a respirator and couldn't talk but waved emphatically her consent. I didn't know that was to be the last time I would see Grandmother Sally alive on this earth.

I treasure the last gift she gave me, and I am reminded that Grandmother was constantly learning and growing spiritually even into her nineties. Walking with God is a constant daily exercise in faith.

7. Exclaim! Quiet time is a time of encouragement and reju-venation. If you find that it works for you, then take what

you have learned about quiet time and pass it on to your friends. Spread the word. Spread the peace.

Thank you, Lord, for allowing me before Your most holy throne. I yearn to know about You. I need a Word from You.
Through Jesus Christ I pray. Amen.

CHAPTER 4

Strength for the Journey

An Adventure Begins

THERE HAVE BEEN NO ACCIDENTS in my life. God has introduced me to people who have served as guides and mentors. He has put me in situations or allowed situations to happen . . . things that often have been painful. But, out of it, I always have learned lessons.

As I look back over the years of my life, I clearly can see stages of growth. Through my childhood and teens, my life revolved around me. As Bette Midler said in the movie *Beaches,* "Enough about me. What do *you* think about me?"

My sisters, Dorothy and Robin, remember the endless questions I asked them as they were trying to go to sleep at night. "Was he looking at me?" "What was he thinking when he was looking at me?" "Okay, what do you *think* he was thinking when he was looking at me?" I drove my sisters crazy.

At five feet ten inches in high school, I was hardly the belle of the ball. I got up the nerve to ask Leroy to the Sadie Hawkins Day dance. He turned me down. Was it my braces? Flat feet? Acne? Or my impressive height?

Now tall is considered beautiful. Back then the prevailing mood was:

> *I am woman.*
> *You are man.*
> *I am shorter,*
> *So you can be taller than.*

Gee, I hated that song.

Through my twenties, I was career-minded. I moved up the ladder of success from "WXXX Super Triple X plays the best music in the Hub City" to WDAM, an NBC affiliate in East-abuchie, just outside of Hattiesburg, Mississippi. I will always be grateful to the then general manager of WXXX, Jim Cameron, and then general manager of WDAM, the late Marvin Reuben, for giving me, a very awkward newcomer, a chance.

WDAM was also abundantly fair. Cindy Wilson, one of the most dynamic, energetic, and committed journalists I ever had the privilege of working with, and I both were interested in anchoring the weekend news. When we indicated that interest to the news director, Bob Ford, he said, "Okay, you can each anchor on alternate weekends." It was Jim Gibbon, the weathercaster at WDAM, who very patiently taught me the ropes of weathercasting, giving me the lift and encouragement I needed just at the right time.

As fate would have it, one of the weekends I was anchoring, Angela Hill, a premier New Orleans anchor, happened to be passing through Hattiesburg. She saw me on the program and, God bless her, told then-WWL news director Phil Johnson about me. I almost fainted when I returned to my small apartment one evening, picked up the phone, and heard, "This is Phil Johnson of WWL-TV in New Orleans. May I speak to Sally-Ann Roberts?"

"This is she," I squeaked, unable to breathe. He asked for an audition tape and an interview. I am forever thankful to Angela Hill, Phil Johnson, and Mike Early, who took a chance on a young journalist from Eastabuchie, Mississippi. I got the job in New Orleans. That was the first big event of my life in the decade of the twenties.

God, Where Are You?

The next was my marriage to Willie at the age of twenty-four. I thought the biggest gift of the decade would be just a couple of years away. I was wrong. Instead it was my first big disappointment. I couldn't get pregnant.

The gynecologist I consulted was at a loss. I cried every month for four years. Then Willie and I went to a fertility specialist who, by the grace of God, diagnosed the problem, and at the age of thirty, I gave birth to a healthy child. Judith arrived into the world safe and sound. And yet after Judith was born, I cried even more.

I had heard of postpartum blues, but I had no idea that I would one day face this debilitating problem. For two months after Judith was born, I cried almost every day. I was afraid to leave the house for fear I would break down in public. The tears came like the waves of an ocean . . . ebbing one moment and bashing the shore the next.

My family had become so used to my crying that they hardly noticed it anymore. I remember one occasion when Mom and my sisters, Dorothy and Robin, were visiting and suddenly I burst into tears. They kept on talking as if I were not there. They weren't being cruel. They just didn't know how to comfort me. Every time they asked me why I was crying, I said, "I don't know!" I thought I was losing my mind.

The most frightening part of all of this was that I really didn't know why I was crying. Judith was healthy and beautiful in every way.

The doctor told me to continue taking my mega-vitamins and rest as much as possible. He said my body was going through a biological change and the chemical balance soon would be restored. Still I cried.

Then one day I got down on my knees and prayed with all my heart. I begged God to help me. I think my prayer was the same Peter called out to Jesus when he looked at the swirling water beneath his feet and began to sink, "Save me, Lord!"

Shortly after that I was at last able to realize the reason for my tears. I had given birth to a beautiful child whom I could not protect. I could not protect Judith from evil people. I could not protect Judith from the consequences she would face if she made bad decisions. My tears were for Judith.

Thank God I confessed these fears to my dad, because he had an answer. He said, "Sally-Ann, do you think your mother and I have not had the same concerns about you and your sisters and brother? I learned long ago to turn that over to God. I live by, and I have bound you all in, the 27th Psalm."

Dad then got out the Bible and read:

> The Lord is my light and my
> salvation
> Whom shall I fear?
> The Lord is the stronghold of my
> life
> of whom shall I be afraid?
> When evil men advance against me
> to devour my flesh,
> When my enemies and my foes attack
> me,
> they will stumble and fall.
> Though an army besiege me,
> my heart will not fear;
> though war break out against me,
> even then will I be confident.

At last the tears stopped.

The Source of Dad's Peace

My father learned to trust God because his parents taught him the power of prayer. Dad says, "Many times the prayers of my parents and grandparents followed me, and I didn't even know they were following me."

As a pilot in the air force, Dad had a couple of close calls.

Each time he survived mechanical problems and landed safely, my family added another story of God's miraculous grace to the family lore. But nothing compares to the incident that happened back in the 1950s.

My family was stationed at Williams Air Force Base in Chandler, Arizona, when suddenly my dad received orders to transfer to a small radar station in Chandler, Minnesota. My mother was very upset because she suspected that a prejudiced, high-ranking base official had instigated my dad's transfer.

But Dad felt there was no way to appeal, since there was a shortage of certified ground-radar specialists. And, in addition to being a pilot, Dad was a ground-radar specialist.

Leaving a nice house in a nice neighborhood to move to a small radar station in a remote area was just sickening to Mom. Dad, whose first love in the air force was flying, was not happy either at the prospect of being grounded. But they performed their patriotic duty and packed up the family Buick Riviera and headed across the country in the middle of summer with no air conditioning and two whining children.

I was one-and-a-half and Butch was five. Every time my big brother passed a house that looked vacant he would shout, "Stop, Daddy! No one lives there! That can be our house!"

We were all fit to be tied by the time we reached Chandler, Minnesota. But our troubles were far from over. The staff at the small radar station took one look at my dad and said they had no job for him. We had driven all this way for nothing. My dad was told to drive to St. Paul to receive further orders.

In St. Paul, Dad was given another runaround while his wife and children waited in the hot car. My parents tried to find a motel room, but the vacancy signs outside were all no-vacancy signs by the time my dad made it to the front desk. Watching Butch and me suffer made the pain even worse for my parents.

To recap, my mom was convinced that a racially biased high-ranking officer had sent the family on a wild goose chase across the country... where other bigoted officers told them in effect to "get lost" . . . and now with two hot, tired, and confused children in tow, they were told there was "no room at the inn."

These were the worst of times for the Roberts family. But God can send an angel when you least expect it.

A white man approached my dad outside a motel where Dad had just gotten his latest rejection. The man said he had been following my dad and knew what he was going through. He said he was working undercover for the National Association for the Advancement of Colored People, documenting acts of discrimination in St. Paul. He directed my father to a place where we could find lodging for the night. We were very grateful. But my parents did not rest easily that night.

Earlier my mother had called home to check on her parents and had found them in a state of panic. "Where are you?" Grandmother Sally hollered as soon as she heard Lucimarian's voice. Mom explained that the family had gotten transfer orders suddenly to move to Minnesota. "Haven't you seen the news?" Grandmother asked incredulously. My mother was dumbfounded as my grandmother delivered the startling news. There had been a plane crash in our old neighborhood.

Piecing it all together, Mom and Dad learned that just hours after we packed up the car and moved out of our house in Chandler, Arizona, a jet had crashed into the neighborhood. It had plowed into houses across the street in the afternoon as children played outside. Butch ordinarily would have been among those children. But for reasons we still find baffling, Butch and all of us were safely on our way to Chandler, Minnesota.

A baby was killed and several people were injured. All of our former neighbors were traumatized. They watched in horror as the plane hurtled toward the subdivision. My parents were told there was mass pandemonium as people did not know which way to run to get out of the plane's path. The jet's pilot had bailed out over the desert, thinking the plane would crash in an unpopulated area.

One of our former neighbors told my mom later that the only humor the people found that night was tracking into the Roberts' former house that had become a shelter for the families who were left homeless. They laughed thinking of the fit Lucimarian would have had if she could have seen the mess they made of the floors she had spent hours on her hands and knees polishing to the required military shine.

We left Chandler, Arizona, kicking and screaming. We knew we would miss our nice little neighborhood in the desert. But we ended up missing a nightmare. Why was our family spared? That is a mystery that will be solved only when we see our Master face to face.

My father has experienced many inexplicable events in his life. That is why he can speak with such blessed assurance. He believes we must trust God in all things.

God's Grace Sustains

My thirties were years of joy, and pain. The birth of Kelly was the high point. The miscarriage of our third child was the indescribably lowest point.

I thought the ultrasound test was taking a little too long. The technician left the room and then returned with her supervisor. After careful examination, he broke the news to me that the fetus had failed to thrive. I drove home as an alien voice wailed. I was alone.

After I had calmed down, I had to admit that from the beginning the news of my pregnancy had been surprising. I always felt that the Lord wanted Willie and me to adopt our third child. But when I got pregnant, I thought I misunderstood God's intentions for our family. Now I was left with confusion. What was going on? Why wasn't the child I carried inside my womb allowed to live? There are many questions that remain unanswered in this life. But as Larnelle Harris sings, "He goes beyond what I can see."

Forty Is Something

When I turned forty, it was as if firecrackers had begun to explode. I felt a need to stop talking and start doing the things God had placed on my heart years ago. I continued to feel God's pulling on my heart to adopt. I knew there were many children in need of homes. Years earlier I had worked on a television series entitled "Who's Watching the Children?"

The series was prompted by a story that fell into my lap. A news photographer and I were on our way to cover a feature story when the assignment editor radioed us to check out a disturbance going on nearby. When we arrived we found that police were taking several children into protective custody.

The children had been living in squalor. Neighbors told me these children repeatedly had come to their houses begging for food. The mother apparently was mentally incompetent. This was one of the few stories I have covered as a reporter that caused me to weep on the job. And I continued crying for days every time I thought about those children wearing ill-fitting clothes sobbing because they were being separated from their mother.

I called the Department of Social Services to find out what would become of the children, and I learned that there is a severe shortage of adoptive and foster homes. I decided to do a news series on the problem. But I knew that was not enough. God was calling me to do more.

Jeremiah Son

At first, my husband, Willie, was less than thrilled with the idea of adoption. He said we had our hands full with two children. There was no way I was going to adopt a child without Willie's full commitment, and so I prayed. I said simply, "Lord, if it is truly Your will for us to adopt, then change Willie's heart." And miraculously He did.

Willie eagerly participated in the ten weeks of training. And my work schedule miraculously changed as well, giving me the time to take the classes. Everything fit perfectly into place. Our fantastic neighbors, the Jordans and the Millses, graciously agreed to babysit with Judith and Kelly. Then the training ended and the application forms, reference letters, and home visits were all completed. And nothing happened.

For a year and a half we waited. But God's voice was clear. "Be still and know I am in charge." Then one day the phone rang.

I was in my office working late one afternoon when Josie Thompson, the social worker, called and said, "Your baby is here." For a moment I thought, what baby? Then when it finally hit me that the waiting was over, I asked breathlessly when we would be able to have him. And Josie said, "Tomorrow afternoon."

"Tomorrow!" I had been told it would happen like this. That when the baby arrived, we would not be given much advance notice. I called Willie, and his old reservations surfaced. "Sally-Ann, we're too old to take care of a baby. We are in our forties, for heaven's sake."

After I hung up, I prayed again that Willie's heart would be softened. God worked quickly. Willie says that he went home after getting my call and impulsively turned on the television set. "The Angela Show" was on, and on that particular day talk show host Angela Hill was talking to adults who had been taken in by loving families as children. They talked about what their foster parents had meant to them. Willie was so moved that he called Angela to thank her for helping him to see the light.

Adopting Jeremiah made no earthly sense. Our friends and relatives were kind, but it was clear they thought we had lost our minds. Here we were in our forties with demanding careers and children and we were about to have a new baby. Willie's co-workers asked him what the baby looked like, and Willie said he had no idea. We had never laid eyes on him.

"What?!" His co-workers were astonished. How in the world

could we adopt a child sight unseen? But I knew Jeremiah was chosen for us by God. He was as much our child as the two to whom I had given birth. Jeremiah came to this earth on a mission from God...a mission that according to God's will could best be accomplished as our son. I thank God for entrusting Jeremiah to our care, just as I thank Him for entrusting Judith and Kelly to our care.

The next day a social worker appropriately named Grace brought Jeremiah to our house. I expected the four-week-old child to be groggy, but Jeremiah son was all eyes, and we immediately bonded. Willie told me soon after Jeremiah's arrival, "I love him. I really love him."

Just as God brought Jeremiah into our lives, He has brought some other surprising people into my life since I turned forty. This is truly turning into the most amazing decade of my life.

God Moves!

In July of 1993 I wrote down goals that were inspired by God. One was the creation of a teen magazine for and by teenagers. Another was the organization called Each One Save One. Before the end of the month, God brought two people into my life who made those dreams a reality.

First, there was Josie Thompson, the social worker who helped us through the adoption process. One day while Josie was conducting a home visit, a young neighbor stopped by the house.

The teenager said he heard me speak at his school about the need for students to find mentors in their chosen professions. He said he wanted to be a veterinarian and asked if I knew of anyone who might be able to guide him. I referred him to Dr. George Robinson, a local veterinarian who ended up hiring the teenager for the summer.

The young man had never been to my house before, nor has he been back since. And I believe his visit on that particular day was orchestrated by God. His visit caused my conversation with Josie to shift directions.

I told her how much I wanted to meet with teenagers at the library on Saturdays to help them plan their future. Josie said she would love to work on that project with me and said that her husband, who was assistant principal of Carver High School, already had a project called The Journalistic Writing Way. To make a long story short, I teamed up with John and Josie Thompson to produce a magazine called *New Generation.*

That magazine was a miracle of God. He brought so many people together to work on it. It was the publisher of Spectrum Unlimited, Bill Bowers, who actually underwrote the initial publication cost.

At about that same time, I felt the need to hold a prayer meeting at my house. My friend Karin Hopkins told me to stop talking about it and just do it. She suggested that I call some friends and invite them. One woman, Cathy Coleman, kept popping into my mind. It made no earthly sense to call Cathy. I barely knew her, but on impulse I called her office and got her on the first try. I later learned that was the first miracle. Cathy was constantly on the go.

I said, "Cathy, I know you don't know me very well, but I'm having a few friends over to the house on Saturday for prayer and Bible study and I was hoping you could come."

Cathy told me that she had married Ray Harris not long ago and that she and Ray spent Saturdays together. I was about to say, "Okay, bye," when suddenly Cathy said, "But I want to talk to you about a mentorship program Ray and I have."

I couldn't believe it. I hurriedly interrupted, "I want to talk to you about Each One Save One." No-nonsense Cathy responded, "Let's do lunch." During our luncheon at Praline Connection, Cathy and I made a lifetime connection. Each One Save One was born.

I know a lot of people dread getting older, but I am looking forward with anticipation to the adventure that lies ahead. I thank God for giving me the strength for the journey thus far, and I trust Him to see me, my family, and my friends the rest of the way home.

Lord,

Thank You for the adventurous life You have planned for me. I pray that I will walk in lockstep with the Holy Spirit.

Through Jesus Christ I pray. Amen.

LIFE LESSON #4
Walk with Angel Vision

Expect a Miracle

Expect a miracle each day. God doesn't take any of our time for granted. As the Bible says, we cannot count the number of times each day we are on God's mind. He is guiding us every single day.

Often when we think of special days we think of Thanksgiving, Christmas, Easter, and other holidays. But every day is a special day when we are walking with angel vision. God knows our time on this earth is limited. Only He knows how limited. There is work for us to do every day. There are lessons for us to learn every day, and there are lessons for us to teach every day. While we schedule our days around our work and our family on the human level, God is scheduling our days on a spiritual level. He is bringing people across our paths each day for a greater purpose. We should not take those who cross our path for granted. That person is there to give or receive. When we walk with angel vision our days are filled with excitement. We wonder what is waiting for us around the corner. The person who is standing beside us in the check-out line may need a word of encouragement from us or may be there to provide us with a word of encouragement or a new insight. The situations that we encounter in the workplace may teach us lessons in patience or test our courage to stand for our convictions.

When we turn our lives over to God and accept His will for our lives, everything that comes to us, good or bad, passes through God first. And He can take what was meant for evil and turn it into good. When we accept God as our Father, we set the wheels in motion for a greater mission than we can even begin to imagine. We may not be able to understand initially how

God is using us or where He is taking us, but rest assured the Holy Spirit is moving us toward our goal.

Accept the Challenge

As Isa. 55:9 says, "As the heavens are higher than the earth, so are my ways higher than your ways and my thoughts than your thoughts." God is magnificently complex. His timing is perfect. He will put you in touch with the people you need to work with to accomplish the mission that He has established. But we have to stay in tune with the Holy Spirit, and that is why Life Lesson #3 is crucial. We have to walk in the spirit so that we will be able to act on spiritual inspirations. When we are in touch with the Holy Spirit we know that we should not ignore thoughts that come into our mind or impulses that God has laid on our hearts. In every situation we ask the question, "Lord, what am I to learn from this? How am I to respond to this situation? What would You have me do?"

Be watchful and mindful. God speaks to us through people and will bring about situations that will help us grow. One of my favorite Stephen Curtis Chapman songs carries this message: "Saddle up your horses / we got a trail to blaze / across the wild blue yonder / of God's amazing grace." How exciting it is to know that each day God is working in us, through us, around us, and for us.

Lord,

Help me to walk with angel vision today so that I will not miss the angels You are bringing across my path. Lord, please help me to be an angel to those You call me to serve.

Through Jesus Christ I pray. Amen.

CHAPTER 5

The Fire Within

The Tollivers

IT WAS A WARM SUMMER EVENING in Akron, Ohio, and yet smoke curled from the chimney of the house at 492 Lucy Street. For the Tollivers who lived there, the smoke was a clear and embarrassing signal to their neighbors that they were one step from the poor house. The year was 1931, and the depression had devastated the Tolliver family.

William Tolliver had lost his garage business. He turned to alcohol to soothe his pain. William managed to get a job at the Goodyear plant, but alcoholism is a hard thing to hide. He lost the job because of his drinking. William's wife, Sally, worked as a maid, a cook, a babysitter—whatever work she could find. A dollar a day was all she earned, but a lot of people were competing for those menial jobs, so work was hard to find.

On this particular summer evening, Sally was cooking dinner for the family on a potbelly stove in the basement. All the utilities in the house, the electricity, the gas, and the water, had been cut off because the family could no longer afford to pay for them. Sally, William, and their three children William, Depholia, and Lucimarian sat at the makeshift dining room table in the basement surrounded by the glow of a kerosene lamp.

Evidently Lucimarian, a precocious six-year-old girl, sensed her parents' foul mood and decided she would do something to help. In her high-pitched voice she chimed, "I have a little song in my heart and I'm going to sing it." "Not at this table you're not!" her father roared. "Just be quiet and eat your dinner!" The unemployed and alcoholic William loved his daughter, but who could be interested in music at a time like this?

Unintimidated by her father's gruffness, Lucimarian gobbled down her dinner and raced outside. When she reached the basement window, she sank to her knees and proceeded to serenade the family through the screen window.

It is that indomitable spirit—that ability to sing in the midst of the storm—that carried Lucimarian to unimaginable heights. Today, Lucimarian is a polished woman whose credentials are awe-inspiring. She was the first woman to serve as president of the Mississippi Coast Coliseum Commission in Biloxi, Mississippi, the first woman to chair the Mississippi State Board of Education, the first woman to serve as a member of the board of directors of the Mississippi Power Company.

At this writing, Lucimarian serves as chairman of the Federal Reserve Bank of Atlanta, New Orleans Branch, and is a member of the board of directors of the Presbyterian (USA) Investment Loan Program. A past vice-chairperson of the Self-Development of People Committee, Lucimarian has traveled to Egypt, Guatemala, Puerto Rico, and other areas in America and abroad to help people help themselves. She is also my mother.

Yet this is Lucimarian Tolliver . . . the same person who used to try to hide her father's shoes so he wouldn't go out drinking at night . . . the same Lucimarian who helped her mother clean houses during the summers . . . the same Lucimarian who wept when there were no presents one Christmas . . . the same Lucimarian whose parents never went beyond the sixth grade in school. Yet Lucimarian Tolliver graduated from college and became a teacher and a social worker. How did she rise from poverty to prosperity?

Each One Save One

That was the question I asked my mother years ago when I was concerned about the cycle of poverty that entangles so many. I told my mother that if we could bottle the solution that helped her and so many others to rise, we could save lives. Mom said simply if she were to start a program she would call it "Each One Save One."

Mom said she was able to make it because of the prayers of her family and the answers to prayers that came in the form of mentors. She said that she had the benefit of many caring people inside and outside of her family who helped her and encouraged her. One woman who helped her in particular was a woman of German descent named Wilma Schnegg.

Miss Schnegg was the enrichment teacher at Robinson Elementary School in Akron, Ohio. She was not beautiful in appearance, but she glowed with an inner beauty that caused her students to shine. She encouraged young Lucimarian year after year. From elementary school through high school, she was in Lucimarian's corner, telling her to concentrate on making good grades because one day she would go to college. College! Where would Lucimarian get the money for college?

Lucimarian listened to Miss Schnegg and the other encouragers around her and believed she could soar with the eagles. During her senior year of high school, Lucimarian applied for the annual college scholarship offered by the *Akron Beacon Journal*. One Sunday she picked up the newspaper and learned that she had won the scholarship and she was on her way to Howard University in Washington, D.C. The impossible dream had been realized.

But Mom would be the first to tell you that she did not make this climb alone. There were others who had gone ahead of her up the mountain and yet took the time to turn around and lift her and others to a higher place. That is why she says, "Let each one save one."

So often we feel overwhelmed by the problems of the world. How can one person save the world? You can save a child by inspiring that child to have hope and self-discipline. Save a child and you save generations.

A Ripple in the World

Look at the wake created by the lifesaver that was thrown to Lucimarian. In her immediate family, her brother William went to college on the G.I. Bill and became a certified public accountant. Her sister Depholia became a nurse. Her father, my Grandfather Tolliver, turned to Alcoholics Anonymous.

I never knew my grandfather to be a drinker. By the time I was born, he was sober. One of my fondest memories of my grandfather was seeing him reading from the Bible as he ministered to another alcoholic.

There are those who would say William Tolliver would have found Alcoholics Anonymous even had Lucimarian not excelled in life. I'm not so sure. I feel that William was encouraged by seeing his daughter triumph, and it gave him greater confidence that he could do so too. But the story of Miss Schnegg's lifesaver does not end there.

While Lucimarian was in college, she met Lawrence Roberts of Vauxhall, New Jersey. They fell in love and were married after college. They had four children—Lawrence Jr., a stockbroker in Houston, Texas; Dorothy, a master's-level social worker on the Mississippi Gulf Coast; Robin, a sportscaster with ESPN and ABC; and me. Three out of four ain't bad at all. My parents did a marvelous job in passing on their respect for God and in insisting that their children use whatever God-given talents they had to the fullest.

As long as Lucimarian has a descendent on this earth, my family will remember Miss Schnegg and say, thank you. Had it not been for her, a mentor who cared, we would not enjoy the success we do today.

Each One Save One, which I cofounded with the dynamic

Cathy Harris, hopes one day to place thousands of caring adults in the classroom with children who need extra encouragement. I found a poem—I don't know who wrote it—that is now the motto of Each One Save One:

If each saved one
won one,
And each one won,
won one,
What hosts would be won,
when every one won,
had won one.

I pray, Dear Lord, for the strength to be quiet today to hear Your voice clearly.

Through Jesus Christ I pray. Amen.

LIFE LESSON #5
Be a Blessing

Let It Begin with Me

The happiest people in life have learned that it is truly a blessing to be a blessing. So many people wrap themselves up in things they think will make them happy and wind up feeling empty. There is a trite, but true, saying, "It is better to give than to receive." If you are feeling down, if you are suffering from low self-esteem, if you feel empty, then it is time to be a blessing.

There are so many people who need you, who would give anything to feel loved. There are countless organizations that are searching for volunteers, whether they are children's organizations such as Big Brothers/Big Sisters and Each One Save One or organizations that care for the homeless such as the Salvation Army and Covenant House.

There are volunteers who spend their time cradling babies who are dying of AIDS. There are volunteers who carry meals to elderly shut-ins. You will find volunteers in schools, hospitals, and nursing homes, and you will find them in every neighborhood.

Follow Your Heart

You don't have to belong to an organization to be a blessing. We can be a blessing wherever we are. One of the most touching stories I ever heard was about an elderly woman who cared for children in her neighborhood. Every day she would go out to the school bus stop and brush the hair of children who were unkempt. She carried damp wash cloths with her to wipe their faces. She looked out of her window and saw a need and decided to fill it. She saw children in her neighborhood who were going off to school each day unkempt and uncared for. And that broke her heart. She wanted the children to know that someone cared.

She became a grandmother to all of the children who passed by her house. She took great interest in seeing their report cards, praising when praise was earned, and encouraging improvement when that was warranted.

Although I never met this woman (I only heard of her legendary giving) I know she must have been a very happy woman. I also know that her giving was not in vain. There were children who might have slipped through the cracks of society unnoticed but instead were lifted to a higher plane.

I do believe that life is a boomerang. What you give eventually comes back to you in some form. If you want happiness, make someone else happy. If you look back on your life, you will probably be able to remember many people who played some role in helping you along the way. Now you can help someone else.

We can all have richer lives if we are willing to give as we have received. God blesses those who allow His blessings to flow through them to others. As long as we are a blessing, we will be blessed. But the minute we close our hands and our hearts, God's blessings will stop.

Any success I have attained in life was possible only because someone cared about a little girl named Lucimarian. And just as Miss Schnegg's legacy will live on through Lucimarian's descendents, we each have the power to impact positively on generations. Most of us will never have a building or a statue dedicated in our honor. But that tribute pales in comparison to the awesome satisfaction of hearing our Savior one day say, "Well done, my good and faithful servant. Well done."

As the old hymn goes

> *If I can help somebody as I pass along,*
> *if I can help somebody with a word or song,*
> *if I can help somebody who is traveling wrong,*
> *then my living will not be in vain.*

Lord,

Please give me the will and the wisdom to be a blessing today. Allow Your love to pour through me as I pass along.

Through Jesus Christ I pray. Amen.

CHAPTER 6

How Great Thou Art

GOD CREATED HEAVEN AND EARTH and everything above and below. Every now and then we should stop and look at the sky, the earth, and the water and then look at our hands and realize that the same God that created all that we admire also created us. We are His greatest treasure. Sometimes we forget and take our eyes off God and look instead at problems that seem insurmountable. But as we gaze upon the beauty of this earth, we realize that the One who carved the canyons and poured forth the seas and built the mountains is more than capable of handling *anything* that we face.

Don Westbrook is an accomplished weathercaster, but as the following pages demonstrate, he is also an equally accomplished photographer. Gaze upon the images that he has captured and know His peace.

Grand Teton National Park, Wyoming

"He makes me lie down in
green pastures,
he leads me beside quiet
waters,
he restores my soul.
He guides me in paths of
righteousness
for his name's sake."
Ps. 23:2, 3

"How priceless is your
unfailing love!
Both high and low
among men
find refuge in the shadow
of your wings,
They feast on the
abundance of your house;
you give them drink from
your river of delights."
Ps. 36:7, 8

Yellowstone National Park

New Smyrna Beach, Florida

"Praise the Lord.
Praise, O servants of the Lord,
praise the name of the Lord.
Let the name of the Lord be praised,
both now and forevermore.
From the rising of the sun to the place where it sets,
the name of the Lord is to be praised.
The Lord is exalted over all the nations,
his glory above the heavens.
Who is like the Lord our God,
the One who sits enthroned on high."
Ps. 113:1-5

"The Lord is my light and
my salvation—
whom shall I fear?
The Lord is the stronghold
of my life—
of whom shall I be afraid?"
Ps. 27:1

New Smyrna Beach, Florida

"As a deer longs for
flowing streams,
so my soul longs for You,
O God.
My soul thirsts for God,
for the living God."
Ps. 42:1, 2

Lewis Lake—Yellowstone National Park

Yellowstone River, Wyoming

"The Lord is my rock, my fortress and my deliverer;
my God is my rock, in whom I take refuge.
He is my shield and the horn of my salvation, my stronghold.
I call to the Lord, who is worthy of praise,
and I am saved from my enemies."
Ps. 18:2, 3

Old Faithful Geyser
Yellowstone National Park

"O Lord, our Lord,
how majestic is your name in
all the earth!
You have set your glory
above the heavens."
Ps. 8:1

"It is God who arms me
with strength
and makes my way perfect.
He makes me feel like
the feet of a deer;
he enables me to stand
on the heights.
He trains my hands for battle;
my arms can bend a
bow of bronze.
You give me your
shield of victory,
and your right hand
sustains me;
you stoop down to make
me great."
Ps. 18:32-35

Yellowstone River—Lower Falls

New Smyrna Beach, Florida

"Be still, and know that
I am God."
Ps. 46:10a

"I lift my eyes to the hills—
where does my help
come from?
My help comes from
the Lord,
the Maker of heaven
and earth."
Ps. 121:1, 2

Yellowstone River—Lower Falls

Grand Teton National Park, Wyoming

"The Lord is my shepherd,
I shall not be in want.
He makes me lie down
in green pastures,
he leads me beside quiet waters,
he restores my soul.
He guides me in the paths of righteousness
for his name's sake.
Even though I walk through the valley
of the shadow of death,
I will fear no evil,
for you are with me;
your rod and your staff, they comfort me.
You prepare a table before me in
the presence of my enemies.
You anoint my head with oil;
my cup overflows.
Surely goodness and love will follow me
all the days of my life,
and I will dwell in the house of the Lord
forever."
Psalm 23

Dear Lord God Almighty, Maker of heaven and earth and all that is good!

Thank You for Your lovingkindness and all of Your wonderful deeds!

Thy tender mercies endure forever!

Through Jesus Christ I pray. Amen.

LIFE LESSON #6
Pray, Prepare, Proceed

Prayer is the first element of any successful plan. We must, as discussed in Life Lesson #3, find time to pray each and every day. We must go into our closets to seek God's face, to ask His guidance, and to gain strength to face what lies ahead. In Mark 1:35 we read, "The next morning he was up long before daybreak and went out alone into the wilderness to pray." If Jesus found it necessary to pray, how much more important then is it for us to pray regularly.

You have a mission. You were born to achieve something great. The question is, what is your mission? What does God want you to do with the time you have remaining on this earth? If you study the life of Dr. Martin Luther King, Jr., you will find that his life exemplified a three-P formula: pray, prepare, proceed.

Pray

Dr. King was a praying man. He sought his Father's guidance. We know that any earthly father would eagerly answer the questions of his child. Good earthly fathers, even though they are only human, do not seek to confuse their children but want to direct them properly. So how much more does our perfect heavenly Father want to direct our paths? We have to ask, and then the answers will begin to come.

The answers will come in the form of ideas and positive thoughts. God speaks to us through our thoughts. Of course, we know the devil can also speak to us through our thoughts. That is why we must stay close to God, so we can discern His will.

Prepare

The second "P" is for prepare. Dr. King obediently prepared

himself for his awesome mission of righting a terrible wrong in this country. He was a well-read man and a student of theology. Dr. King began preparing as a child by doing the work even before he could possibly understand the importance of that work. Dr. King was an articulate speaker and persuasive writer. These qualities didn't just happen. They were the product of years of preparation. We, too, must yield ourselves to the Potter's hand and do the work to prepare our hearts, minds, and bodies for the mission.

Proceed

Finally, we must have the courage to proceed. Opportunities arose in Dr. King's life that may have seemed coincidental. Why was he in Montgomery at just the moment in history when Rosa Parks refused to give up her seat on a public bus? Why of all the ministers in Montgomery was Dr. King chosen to lead the boycott even though he was a new minister in town? Some would say these were acts of fate. I say they were acts of faith. Dr. King was where he was because he trusted and obeyed God.

If we trust and obey God, He will lead us to places that we cannot begin to imagine. That is not to say that we have all been entrusted with a mission that will bring us worldwide acclaim, as in the case of Dr. King. There are many people, unnoticed on earth, who are being cheered on by the angels in heaven because they are doing what God has called them to do. The Bible says that you cannot give a cup of water to a child without its being noticed by our heavenly Father. From God's perspective, none of His workers are insignificant.

You have been given a tremendous mission to touch lives. If you do not do what you are called to do, it will not get done. If Dr. King had been disobedient or had lacked faith or courage, where would this country be today? We cannot assume that someone else would have picked up the mantle. We can thank God that Dr. King did not disobey. But are we going to obey? The rewards and potential consequences are great.

Trust and Obey

Proceeding is the most difficult part of this formula. It often requires us to step out completely on faith, with nothing visible to substantiate that faith. Birds cannot fly by clinging to the limb. There comes a time in our lives when we have to let go and let God. Throughout the Bible can be found examples of God working extraordinary feats in the lives of ordinary people. And each of those people expressed doubts about their ability to proceed. They were afraid. Jeremiah said, I'm too young. Esther said, I can't go before the king unannounced. Moses said, I'm a stutterer. In anointing David, a shepherd boy, to be king of Israel, the Lord explained to His prophet Samuel in I Sam. 16:7, "Don't judge by a man's face or height . . . I don't make decisions the way you do! Men judge by outward appearance, but I look at a man's thoughts and intentions."

To the world, you may appear to be nothing but a poor shepherd with no discernable strengths, but that should not stop you from doing what God has put on your heart. It may be true that you cannot accomplish great goals, but our great Father can accomplish those goals through you. The time will come when your name will be called. Opportunities will arise suddenly, calling upon you to act. You have no way of knowing when that time will come. But remain prayerful and continue preparing until that time comes.

Moses was at the edge of the Red Sea with an Egyptian army in hot pursuit. The people whom Moses led out of Egypt were in panic, crying out, "Have you brought us out here to die in the desert because there were not enough graves for us in Egypt? Why did you make us leave Egypt?" (Exod. 14:11). Moses' faith was put to the test. He began to pray. Then in Exod. 14:15, we read, "The Lord said to Moses, 'Quit praying and get the people moving! Forward, march!'" The rest is history.

Pray! Prepare! Proceed! You are a child of the living King.

Forward, march!

   Please, Lord, give me courage and confidence to complete the mission You have assigned to me. Lead me, Lord. I am Yours.

   Through Jesus Christ I pray. Amen.

CHAPTER 7

Beyond the Fence

UPTOWN NEW ORLEANS HAS TREES OF EVERY DESCRIPTION reaching high, bending low, branches intertwined, providing huge sombreros for protection from the harsh, sweat-popping rays of the sun. I traveled the same route every day to pick up my daughter Judith from school.

I was enchanted by the mysterious charm among the light and shadows, the heat, and the occasional cool breezes from the river. There are many fences Uptown—pretty little picket fences, threatening barbed-wire-topped fences, brick fences lined with ferns and climbing vines.

Sometimes behind even the tallest fence I can catch a glimpse of what is behind it. They are beautiful oases for the homeowners fortunate enough to afford them.

The message is clear: stay out! The guard signs posted along the front hedge indicate that alarms will sound and the police will come to deal with any unwanted guests. Such is life in the 1990s.

Murders, burglaries, car thefts, assaults, and the various assortment of other crimes make many feel the family fortresses are a necessity, not a luxury.

Fences are nothing new, however. They have always existed. How else would we know what's mine and what's yours? My grandparents on Lucy Street in Akron, Ohio, had a backyard fence, or maybe it was their neighbors' fence. I don't know who put it up. It was just there.

I can remember standing alone in the backyard and wondering who lived behind the back fence. It was so quiet over there, and mysterious. I was too lazy, though, to walk down the long hill, around the corner, and up the other side of the steep hill to introduce myself to the people who lived there. And I didn't dare climb over the fence. To do so would risk both the unknown and the known. Both were frightening prospects.

I didn't know what the neighbors would do to me for coming on to their property uninvited, but I knew that if my grandmother caught me climbing over that fence, I'd catch hello. So the backyard mystery was never solved.

But it's not the fencing around houses that concerns me, but rather the fences around people.

I'm trying to break down my fence. It isn't easy. Fear is a hard brick to crack. It takes courage to be real. It takes courage to extend the hand of friendship to those who live in different neighborhoods. Will I be rejected? Will my friendship be abused? It's easier just to play it safe and stay in familiar surroundings with familiar people. It is easier to judge people in a five-second glance to determine whether they fit my prerequisite age, race, social, and educational qualifications. But I know now I cannot truly live a full and rich life behind a fence.

Building the Fence

I don't know exactly when I started to build the fence. When I was a child in Sioux City, Iowa, there were very few black children, and race didn't seem to matter to me and my friends anyway. I wasn't even aware of being different from them.

My mother told me years later, however, that while my

playmates and I didn't notice my race, adults did. Once, at a parade in Sioux City, my mother said she beamed with pride as I stood, back straight, and saluted the flag as it passed. But as she looked around, her pride turned to shock as she saw white adults frowning at me with disdain.

My parents tried to protect me and my sisters and brother as best they could from the discrimination and racial hatred that permeated the America of our childhood. My brother, Butch, and I saw separate water fountains for the first time in a Montgomery, Alabama, department store. Butch ran up eagerly to the water fountain that was labeled "colored," but he walked away disappointed. He sulked, "That is just plain ol' water. It isn't colored."

We traveled a lot during my childhood. My father was an officer in the air force. After being stationed in Sioux City, we moved to Tuskegee, Alabama. My father, who had been a Tuskegee airman, returned to Tuskegee Institute as an Air Force Reserve Officer Training Corps instructor.

It was 1958 and the Civil Rights movement was just getting under way. I did not understand the intricacies of racial hatred. All I understood was that a hamburger restaurant that I yearned to visit was off limits to me because my parents pointed out there was a sign in the window that read Whites Only.

I attended Chambliss Children's House, a segregated elementary school. What the school lacked in updated facilities and textbooks, it more than made up for in pride and compassion.

These were formative years for me. I learned that there were two communities—one for whites and one for Negroes. From Tuskegee we moved to Akron, Ohio, which boasted of integrated schools and public accommodations. But I found out that the North and the South were very much alike in racial animosity. In the South, you knew immediately where you stood. In the North, you found out quickly enough.

The integrated schools in Akron were neighborhood

schools. The neighborhoods were segregated, so the schools were too. I can remember my parents stopping at a house that had a For Sale sign in front of it. My mother got out to inquire, but quickly returned. She said that the house was no longer for sale. While we did not discuss the matter, we all knew the house was not for sale . . . to people like us.

In the early 1960s my family moved to New Jersey, where the racial climate was better. At the elementary school on the air force base, I had white friends for the first time since I had lived in Iowa. But once I entered the teen years, I felt that black pride meant being with my brothers and sisters.

I didn't know then, as I do now, that friendships should be based on spirit, not color. Even so, I was very close to Joy Throm. I overlooked the fact that she was white because she was the only American girl my age in my neighborhood in a suburb just outside of Izmir, Turkey, where my father was stationed. Joy lived upstairs in my apartment complex, and she was a joy to be around. We passed many an evening laughing, eating popcorn, and chewing the fat. Since Izmir had no television at the time, and only one American radio station, we had plenty of time to talk.

I was also close to Mich, a bilingual Turkish girl who lived down the street. She reminded me a lot of my cousin Cheryl. Even though Cheryl lived in Akron, Ohio, far from the Aegean coast, Mich and Cheryl were very much alike. I would have had more Turkish friends if I had learned the language.

I wasn't able to cross the language fence, so there were many great spirits I never met in Turkey.

One of the American children's greatest pastimes while abroad was to dream of going home to the United States. We yearned to eat a Big Mac and french fries again. We wondered about the television shows we were missing.

We oohed and aahed every time a friend announced that his or her family had received transfer orders. "Where ya going?" we'd all want to know. "McClellan Air Force Base, in

California." Ooh! "McGuire Air Force Base, in New Jersey." Aah!

Then my father got his transfer orders. "Where are we going?!" I screamed. "Keesler Air Force Base, in Biloxi, Mississippi," he replied. I cried.

"Mississippi! That's where they lynch black people!" I protested. It didn't help matters that at the nearby base theater a rerun of *In the Heat of the Night* was currently being shown. After seeing the movie, I was more terrified than ever—or should I say more angry than ever.

My friends' reaction was predictable: derisive laughter. "Mississippi? You might as well stay here."

My parents told me that my apprehensions were ridiculous. But all I could see was the Ku Klux Klan greeting the airplane in white sheets and laying down the code of behavior they expected from us colored folk. Little did I know that we had more to fear from Mother Nature than from man's evil nature.

We arrived in Biloxi in July of 1969, just in time to greet Hurricane Camille. Camille was truly a nondiscriminatory calamity. Rich and poor, black and white counted their losses and buried their dead.

Through it all, I noticed a spirit of community, as good people of all races reached out to help one another. The Mississippi Gulf Coast, I learned, had some mighty fine people who didn't deserve my preconceived stereotyping.

At that time, Biloxi still had two high schools. Biloxi High was predominantly white, and Nichols High was all black. My parents, over my objections, decided I would attend Biloxi High School with the other children from the base.

I was in the eleventh grade. I cannot remember having any close white friends—not because of anything specifically said or done by white students. Our fences were up. They felt comfortable among themselves, and I felt more comfortable being around the few other blacks attending Biloxi High. Besides small talk, I could not see any reason to socialize outside my race.

The next year, Nichols High School became a junior high and Biloxi High became the only public high school in town. The merger brought on new tensions, an "us-against-them" mentality that was most evident at pep rallies and athletic events.

When the school band hit the first note of "Dixie," the battle lines were drawn. White students cheered and black students booed, raising the black-power fist in defiance. More bricks were added to my fence.

After graduation, my closest friends and I enrolled at the University of Southern Mississippi in Hattiesburg. Since room assignments were based on personal preferences whenever possible, most students roomed with people of the same race.

My best friends from high school, Gloria Otis and Doris Thomas, made great roommates. We had a blast. Again through college, except for small talk and friendly classroom repartee, I had no meaningful relationships outside of my race. I don't know how many great spirits I missed during college.

Bringing It Down

After college, the fence stayed up. I had only a couple of friends outside my race. My sisters and parents on the other hand always had, and still have, close friends who happen to be white. For some reason, they never erected barriers of race. They have always felt equally inclined to visit or accept into their homes people without regard for race.

So what happened to me? We all dealt with the same circumstances. We all had scars from the past. Yet their scars were less evident than mine. Why, when a new black female co-worker arrived in town, would I go out of my way to befriend her and invite her to my home, and not do the same for a white co-worker?

It all boiled down to trust. I did not trust. I did not want to risk being hurt or being judged by people who may have preconceived ideas of who I am because I am black. Black folks know black folks are just folks, but I did not trust white folks to know that. Because so many people have not lived around or socialized with people outside their own race, there is sometimes deep-rooted ignorance about the people who live on the other side of the fence.

We don't know each other. We still haven't learned that what Maya Angelou wrote in *Human Family* is true: "We are more alike, my friend, than we are unalike."

I am still in the process of breaking down the wall that has held me in and others out for so many years. I'm hoping it will not take as long to demolish as it did to build.

I have role models around me who, by the grace of God, are leading the demolition crew. I can point to people such as Cathy Harris, who grew up in the Desire Housing Development. When she invited me to a New Year's Eve party at her home years ago, I was surprised to see that half of the people there were white. Even more surprising, they truly seemed to have been friends for quite some time . . . real friends.

Cathy is a person who judges people by their character. She gives others the benefit of the doubt that they will judge her the same way. She counts among her best friends bus drivers and business executives. Cathy learned awhile back that God put good people everywhere.

Pattie Shoener is another member of the demolition crew. She grew up in a small Pennsylvania town where there were no black people. But when I look at Pattie, I don't see color. I see sister. I trust her and feel comfortable around her.

Through the mentoring organization Each One Save One that Cathy and I founded, we have found many kindred spirits who are just plain good folks. The multiracial board of men and women has one objective: to bring out the best in children . . . all children, regardless of race. When I look around the table at those gathered for our regular planning sessions and look at the mentors, I don't even notice race. Instead, I see their commitment. They are my brothers and sisters.

As I am working to bring down my wall, you, too, are perhaps working to do the same. I know that the only way to succeed ultimately is through prayer. I need something bigger than me to see people as spirit, not human. I need the eyes and ears of God.

My prayer partner, Phyllis, has been my lifeline. We became prayer partners in a most unusual way. Years ago, Phyllis, who is Catholic, visited my Methodist Church Sunday School. On that particular Sunday, for some reason Brother Harold Seals decided that our class should choose prayer partners. In the first drawing, Phyllis and I were not matched as prayer partners. But the drawing was done over again because a mistake had been made. The next time Phyllis drew my name. It was her first and last time to visit my Sunday School class. And we have been prayer partners ever since.

Since 1990, on almost a daily basis, Phyllis and I have shared triumphs and tragedies and thanksgiving over the phone with God. Jesus said, "Wherever two or three are gathered in my name, there am I also in the midst of them." Having a prayer partner is one of the best blessings I have received. I thank God for guiding our lives and hearing our prayers.

And we will need God's help if we are to have any chance of helping our children reach their full potential in a multicultural society.

Stopping New Construction

I didn't fully realize how damaging and pervasive fences are among our young people until I attended a rap session with high school seniors. They were part of an Upward Bound college preparatory group. They were very smart kids, but it was clear they still had much to learn.

When the question of race was raised, one black student who attends a predominantly white private school said that she does not socialize with white students because she said every single one of them goes out drinking and carousing every weekend.

Another student said that there are clearly white students who want to be black and black students who want to be white. He said the students in question are always hanging around with people outside of their own race.

When I was growing up, we had cruel terms for a black who didn't fit the definition of black: oreo, Aunt Jemima, wannabee, Uncle Tom. Whites who hung around with blacks could be labeled "N" lover. The "N" word is still too painful even to write.

Many of us ran away from those labels, altering our language to fit the code, eating lunch in the cafeteria only with "our own kind." It was just safer. Today, if you go into many school cafeterias you will find separate enclaves of blacks, whites, Asian Americans, and Hispanics. Apparently, according to my young friends at the rap session, the self-imposed separatism continues today.

We all have built fences for our emotional protection. But the fences themselves are more destructive than anything that could attack them. They are limiting, and we are free. At least, we are supposed to be free.

We hide behind labels: black—white, Republican—Democrat, liberal—conservative, man—woman, Christian—Jew, white collar—blue collar, rich—poor, the list is never-ending. But peel away the labels of nationality, race, gender, religion, and socio-economic level. Peel it all away, and what do you have? Spirits. We are all spirits.

Don't Judge Me by the Suit I'm Wearing

Remember the movie *Cocoon*? The young man is leering through a ship porthole as the woman of his dreams takes off her clothes, unaware of the peeping Tom. As each layer of clothing comes off, the man's eyes get bigger and bigger, but she doesn't stop with her clothes. To his astonishment, the woman begins to shed her skin.

She is an alien in disguise. The man, in terror, runs to tell the ship captain. And horror of horrors, the captain pulls back his eyelid to reveal that he, too, is an alien.

The captain and the young woman were only disguised as human beings. Their true identity was beneath their skin. And so it is with us. We are aliens in this material world. As wise philosophers have said, "We are not human beings having a spiritual experience; we are spiritual beings having a human experience."

Spirits can not be labeled. They just are. We will leave our old bodies behind one day. All the wealth we are able to amass will end up in someone else's hands. Only our spirit will get out of here alive.

The minutiae of this world that seems so important now, all the labels we have added to dignify ourselves or demean others, will not add up to a hill of red beans and rice. At death, the labels go into the ground. The spirit goes on. I will leave it to your religious instructor to instruct you as to where good spirits and evil spirits go.

If we all truly believed that this is not all there is, that we have a Divine Judge who sees all, knows all, and judges all, this world would be a much better place to live. We would have no murders, thefts, lying, cheating, or devilment of any kind, because we would all realize that we are accountable for our actions.

The reason we have the troubles we do today is because many people are living as if this is all there is. They say hurtful things and spew out hateful venom as freely as Mardi Gras revelers throw their beads.

I don't pretend to have all the answers. I'm just a frustrated witness of a society that doesn't make much sense. People live as though they are their labels, and they are not.

I explained it to my daughter Judith like this one morning:

> Suppose the T-shirt you have on right now is the shirt you were given at birth. You didn't choose your shirt. It was chosen for you. You can't exchange it for another color or size or design. You must wear the shirt you were given the

rest of your life. The only thing the shirt is good for is identification, since no two are exactly alike.

Now, here's the question. Are you your shirt? You have to wear the shirt and take care of it. But eventually, even under the best circumstances your shirt will sag and grow gray with age. The question remains, are you your shirt?

Judith answered, "Of course not. I'm underneath it."

Smart girl, that Judith. So it then follows, if we are not our package, why do we act as if we are? Why do we limit ourselves and others to fit a description or a stereotype? It's stupid and it's wrong.

Blessings of the Spirit

Good things happen when we accept ourselves and others as spiritual beings. It is freeing to know that there is a power surging within us that knows no human bounds. When we tap that power, nothing can hold us back.

When we realize that we are more than flesh and blood, then we know that the person staring back at us in the mirror is a mighty spirit in disguise. That is awesome!

In that light, what is age? 40, 50, 65? As long as we're in this suit, we've got work to do . . . hills to climb . . . battles to win. Spirits do not get old. Oh, the suit may not work as well as it used to, but the spirit is as powerful as ever.

Spiritual beings are never homesick. Wherever we are, we are home. Just about anywhere on this planet, you will find kindred spirits to befriend. During my years of traveling with my air force dad, from Arizona, to Iowa, to Ohio, to New Jersey, to Izmir, and finally Mississippi, my family made friends at every stop along the way.

When you recognize that you are a spiritual being, you can more clearly see the needs of others, and you can see what is really important in life.

Saints in Disguise

During my junior year at college in Hattiesburg, Mississippi, I headed home to Biloxi one weekend. My mother had urged me to get an early start, but instead I waited until almost evening to head out on the highway. The stretch of Highway 49 between Hattiesburg and Biloxi is very lovely. There are lots of trees and not much else.

But on this particular Friday, those woods became frightening. Out there in the middle of nowhere, I saw black smoke begin pouring from my car exhaust. The car began slowing to a halt. Just then, I saw a rest-area sign. I turned onto the roadway that curved off the highway. I thought I would find other motorists there, or, better yet, a telephone. Wrong, and wrong again. There were only picnic tables and more trees. My car was dead, and I was alone.

I walked back to the highway to hail a passing motorist. One by one they passed me by. I can still see one large man sitting in a luxury car laughing and talking with his passengers. As I waved frantically, he didn't even glance in my direction. Other cars and trucks zoomed past. I could hardly blame them. With my car out of sight in the rest area, I looked like a hitchhiker.

Finally, a car pulled off the road, and a man got out. His mouth said he wanted to help me, but his eyes said he wanted something else. I asked him to go down the road to find a tow truck to send back for me and my car. But he said he was pretty handy with cars, and he would be happy to take a look at mine. My car was going in reverse when I placed it in drive. I knew that whatever was wrong with my car, it could not be fixed by the side of the road.

When I continued to urge him to go for help, he asked where I was headed. I told him Keesler Air Force Base. Now, what a coincidence. He was heading in the same direction. He offered to give me a ride. (My momma didn't raise no fool.)

I knew I was in trouble. I was in the woods with a strange man as the sun was setting in the west.

Then suddenly just as in some old western, the cavalry came to my rescue. In this case, the cavalry was an old truck, and seated in the cab were a man, a woman, and little girl.

"Miss, can we help you?" the man asked.

You could have knocked me over with a cotton ball. Where did they come from? How did they even know I was up here? I wasn't visible from the highway. But here they were, my heroes.

I asked if they would go to the nearest gas station and send a tow truck. They left, and minutes later returned. The first man was still there. His head was buried beneath the hood of my car—I'm sure it was to keep the family in the truck from getting a good look at him and fingering him in some future police lineup.

The man in the truck said the mechanic was out on a call and that the gas station attendant didn't know when he would return. "I think you should let us take you to the gas station to wait for him," he said. "It's not safe for you to be out here alone at night."

You're telling me. I squeezed into the truck next to the man, his wife, and daughter, grateful to have safe passage away from what could have been my rest "in peace" stop. As he was driving me to the gas station, I asked him why had he stopped for me. He replied, "The truth of the matter is, we saw you hailing cars and we passed you by. But as we got farther down the road, our conscience started bothering us, and we came back for you."

As long as I live, I will never forget that kind family that didn't know me, and yet cared for me. Now that I am older, I realize God was teaching me a lesson that sunset by the side of the road. He was pointing out the fallacy of judging people by their appearance.

The men who stopped for me, the one who rattled my spirit and the one who warmed it, were both white. Saints and demons come in all colors. And, sometimes, saints drive old pickup trucks.

Dear Lord,

Thank You for the angels You send my way. Thank You for those who break down walls of indifference to shed Your light of love. Please, Lord, help me to see with Your eyes and love with Your heart.

Through Jesus Christ I pray. Amen.

LIFE LESSON #7
Don't Let the Devil Tap-Dance on Your Head

As I was writing this lesson, my nine-year-old daughter, Kelly, was angry and crying. I told her that she could not go to the mall with her friends without supervision, and that did not go over too well. Sometimes life's trials come in small packages.

No matter how saintly you are or how much you read the Bible and pray, you are going to face challenges. But that is when you need the power that comes from a deep, abiding relationship with God. When Kelly came into my tiny makeshift office/nursery/guest room/television room, I was more than a little distracted.

There I was, trying to write a lesson about finding peace, and my own peace was being disturbed. I sat quietly for a few minutes after Kelly, in tears, stomped out of the room. I tried to figure out what I should write. I could not find any words. The devil was making too much noise tap-dancing on my head. The small quiet voice that was so evident before was now gone.

Then, without saying a word, my friend Pattie took my hand and began to pray. She asked God to restore my focus and give me the words He would have me to write. As she prayed that simple prayer it was clear that I was to share what was going on at that moment.

We all have Kelly-type challenges to deal with every day. So often it's not the big problems that wear us down, but the little ones. Kelly was a normal nine-year-old, putting her mom through the same paces I once put mine through. Whether at work, at home, on the road, or at school, we are going to face those devilish little situations. And we should deal with them the same way Pattie did . . . pray.

The devil is constantly looking for a chance to get a foothold in our lives. When we are working for God, rest assured the devil is not far away. He wants to distract us, disillusion us, and ultimately derail us. The devil also wants to divide us.

Everywhere we look we see the "us-against-them" mentality. How many wars have been fought through the ages because of hatred! And we see the "us-against-them" mentality continuing to rear its ugly head, even among our young.

One day, there was a school parade in my neighborhood. It was a nice parade but a very short one. I asked why the route had been cut short. I was told that it was to avoid a fight with students from the school down the street. Two high schools only a few miles apart were actually worlds apart. It doesn't take much hate or many haters to build a wall. And if we have enough courage, it will not take many of us to bring it down. But it will take courage.

We first must recognize our own prejudices. If we are honest with ourselves, we will admit that we all have prejudices. We all have wounds and experiences that influence our opinions of others. When we get to heaven we will find there are no races of people, nationalities, or skin colors, only spirits. Until we get to heaven we will have to constantly work at seeing people as spirits. When we feel our old preconceived ideas rearing their ugly heads in our minds, we should remember the Golden Rule given to us by Jesus Christ: "Love your neighbor as yourself." For those of us who are believers, loving one another is not just something we do to further our careers or to win popularity contests. We do it because we have no choice. We are commanded by our Father to love one another.

What about those who treat us badly? The Bible tells us in Matt. 5:44 to love even our enemies and pray for those who persecute us. It doesn't take a special quality to love our friends. Even the most vile fiends can do that. But we are striving to grow spiritually into a peculiar people who can love without expecting anything in return.

Recently I was the victim of an unscrupulous and rude taxi driver. He ended up pocketing a very large tip because he said he didn't have change. Years ago I would have seethed all night about being so abused.

But now I realize that the driver only robbed himself. He is responsible for his actions. I am only responsible for my response. Sooner or later we will all line up for payday, and our Boss, the only true judge, will mete out payment.

When I am confronted by a person who makes me feel uncomfortable, I mentally stop and think "spirit." I have to remind myself that I'm not talking to a person. I'm talking to a fellow spirit on this planet. There can be wonderful revelations when we bring down our walls of prejudice and let someone in. And our prejudice is not always racial. It can be prejudice of age or economic status or educational achievement. I have had some of my most amazing conversations with people who years before I would not have even noticed. God can and does work miracles using unexpected messengers.

The devil on the other hand wants to block those messengers. He wants us to distrust, dislike, and separate ourselves from people who are different.

We need to get the devil off our heads and out of our minds. Don't give the devil even a toehold or he'll move in and make himself right at home. The devil acts through our thoughts. As Isa. 5:20 tells us, he can make good appear bad, and the bitter, sweet. If you want to make the devil happy, then dwell on thoughts of hatred, jealousy, bitterness, discouragement, selfishness, and pessimism. You get the picture. The devil wants to bring us down. In Phil. 4:8 we find the way to fight off the devil as we are instructed to think positive thoughts.

As believers, we are most comfortable talking about God and his goodness. But if we believe in God and His word, then we also know that there is a devil who has been given power for a limited period of time. This life lesson is summed up in Eph. 6:12-18. If we follow this advice, which requires determination and discipline and awareness of just who our enemy is, then we will all be able to keep the devil from tap-dancing on our heads:

For our struggle is not against flesh and blood, but against the rulers, against the authorities, against the powers of this dark world and against the spiritual forces of evil in the heavenly realms. Therefore put on the full armor of God, so that when the day of evil comes, you may be able to stand your ground, and after you have done everything, to stand. Stand firm then, with the belt of truth buckled around your waist, with the breastplate of righteousness in place, and with your feet fitted with the readiness that comes from the gospel of peace. In addition to all this, take up the shield of faith, with which you can extinguish all the flaming arrows of the evil one. Take the helmet of salvation and the sword of the Spirit, which is the word of God. And pray in the Spirit on all occasions with all kinds of prayers and requests. With this in mind, be alert and always keep on praying for all the saints.

Dear Lord,

Please arm me for the battle. You are my Rock. In You I have the victory.

Through Jesus Christ I pray. Amen.

CHAPTER 8

Sometimes You Have to Sing

ONE SUNDAY AFTERNOON IN 1979 I was at home flipping the television dial looking for something interesting to watch. Suddenly I stopped. Something on Channel 12, the public television station, caught my eye. It was an elderly woman talking about her children. Her smile was magnetic. I was even more fascinated when I found out that the woman did not live far from me. Hugh Downs' "Over Easy" television series on that day focused on Lottie Mae Burnley, an Uptown New Orleans resident.

When the show ended I impulsively picked up the telephone book and looked up Mrs. Burnley's telephone number. I dialed, not knowing exactly what I planned to say to her. But when she answered the phone, I found no words were necessary. In an inimitable, raspy voice I have grown to love, Mama Burnley greeted me cheerfully. Mama doesn't know any strangers. People who call her number by accident always find a gregarious, loving friend. These "wrong number" telephone conversations can last for hours and result in friendships that last forever.

"I talk from experience, not books, 'cause I am a third-grade scholar! Ha HAH!" Mama Burnley's spirited, full-bodied laugh is infectious. At age ninety, she has all of the aches and pains associated with an aging body. But her spirit is hardly weary. She still has the eyes of a child that light up with joy at the simplest of things, such as a knock at the door from an old friend or a new old friend. She says, "I ask the Lord not for my wants but for my needs." She knows from experience that He will provide.

We have been friends since that day in 1979. As a full-time employee and mother, I do not call her as often as I should. But she never makes me feel guilty for my failure to call regularly. She says, "This is Mama. I know you are busy. Besides you can pray for me as well in New Orleans East as you can over at my house. I know Sweet Jesus can hear your prayers."

I have learned much about "Sweet Jesus" from Mama Burnley. She says Jesus reached down to her in the depths of her despair one night and took away her desire for alcohol.

"I'd go to the store for whiskey and I'd cry 'Dear Lord, please don't let me buy that whiskey.'" Mama Burnley said that she would go for five months without drinking, and then she would binge for two or three weeks.

One night, she says, she cried, "Dear Lord, take me out of this world." Suddenly, she says, a voice called out, "God saved you from drowning." Mama Burnley was reminded of the accident that had happened nine years earlier.

Mama says she was on a wharf fishing and fell into the water.

> When I came up I was reaching for the rafter, and I heard this voice say, "Lord have mercy on me." It was as if I was supposed to say that. So I said, "Lord have mercy on . . ." but before I could get it out I went down for the second time. When I came up I was by the rafter.

Mama Burnley says she clung to the pier until her brother-in-law was able to pull her to safety.

Remembering that near-drowning experience, Mama Burn-ley realized there is nothing too great for God to do. That night, with her pillow soaked with tears, she called out to the Lord to save her from her sins. And He did. She gave up drinking and has not had a sip of alcohol since 1964.

"I lived in fear when I was in sin," she declares. Ever since Mama Burnley has been free from the sin that imprisoned her, she has tried to show others the way. "I've been where people are. I don't criticize people because I've been there."

Mama Burnley's love comes not from a sense of self-right-eousness, but the knowledge of God's amazing grace. She also warns people not to fall for the tricks of Satan. "You can go to hell so fast you will think you're on roller skates," she says.

Mama Burnley never had any biological children, but she has been blessed with more children than she can count. Her bedroom dresser is filled with the faces of people young and mature, black and white, whom Mama Burnley claims as her children. She prays for them and counsels them and is there for them whenever they need her.

Once Mama Burnley was on an airplane, and the woman sitting next to her was in a quandary whether to accept a job in another city. She did not want to leave home. Mama Burnley advised her, "Sometimes we have to go out of our way to get our blessings." The woman accepted Mama Burnley's advice and has written to her several times to thank her for leading her in the right direction. And Mama Burnley claims her as one of her daughters.

I didn't know the old Lottie Mae Burnley. She loves to testify about how God saved her and made her a new person. The Lottie Mae I know is one who has a song in her heart. She says that when she sits in her little house reading her Bible with a magnifying glass or cooking her much-acclaimed gumbo, she is not alone. She feels the presence of Jesus.

She often sings when no one but Jesus can hear her. Her voice may not be professionally trained, but Leontyne Price never sang with greater feeling than Lottie Mae Burnley.

One of the songs she loves to sing is one the Lord planted in her heart:

> *I'm so glad that I've been changed.*
> *I know the angels in heaven gonna sign my name.*
> *I know when I get up in heaven I can choose my seat and sit down.*
> *I know King Jesus is going to give me a starry crown.*

> *Yes, I know. Oh yes, I know.*

> *I'm so glad that you've been changed.*
> *I know the angels in heaven gonna sign your name.*
> *I know when you get up in heaven you can choose your seat and sit down.*
> *I know King Jesus is going to give you a starry crown.*

> *Yes, I know. Oh yes, I know.*

Mama Burnley is not a hothouse Christian . . . one who is okay only when kept away from the chill of the world. Mama ventures out on faith and with her faith for all to see. She is not worried about political correctness or even how she is treated. Mama's philosophy is simple . . . love can win any battle.

Mama's street is one where whites and blacks and the prosperous and financially challenged live side by side. Mama refuses to look at color or economic status in choosing her friends. She doesn't particularly care if you are even interested in being her friend. If anything, Mama loves a challenge.

There was a man who lived down the street from Mama Burnley who refused to speak to her. He would walk past her and ignore her friendly greeting. But that did not discourage Mama Burnley. She continued to speak cheerfully to the elderly gentleman whenever she saw him, sometimes even shouting a greeting to him down the street.

Eventually the man began to grunt a reluctant response. Slowly that grunt turned into something discernable. And then one day that man started greeting Mama Burnley with all the love and cheerfulness with which she greeted him. She began baking pies for the man and his wife, and they shared many happy times together because Mama Burnley refused to give anything less than love.

Mama has worn down many a hard heart with kindness, but Mama doesn't play when it comes to church. She has been known to quietly pass a piece of paper to someone she spots chewing gum in church. And if someone tries to engage Mama in conversation during the worship service, she nips that in the bud by passing the person her phone number.

One Sunday, Mama Burnley was riding in her church van to Sunday worship service, and an ill-tempered woman got on. The woman was angry with the driver for having picked her up late. So Mama, who could not tolerate unpleasantness on the way to church, stepped in. She told the woman that the driver was doing the best he could. The annoyed woman snapped at Mama, telling her to mind her own business. I asked in great anticipation, "Mama, what did you do?" Mama Burnley replied with a smile, "I started to sing." Mama sang all the way to church. By the time they arrived at the church, everyone on board was filled with the spirit.

Mama Burnley has many talents. She can whip up the most delicious shrimp salad, crawfish étouffée, gumbo, and stuffed mirlitons you have ever tasted in your life. Her beautiful quilt tops are sewn by hand so meticulously that you would think they were machine stitched. Mama loves to show off her ability to thread a needle without the aid of glasses. But her most amazing talent is her ability to sing through the storms of life.

"I talk to Jesus just like I'm talking to you," she explains. "I have conversations with Jesus, and I wait for Him to answer." Mama Burnley is not alone, and she is not lonely. When she goes to bed at night she rests peacefully. "I look up and I'm smiling, and it seems like He ought to be right there on the wall. I always remember to say, 'Good night, Sweet Jesus.'"

Thank You, Lord, for the Mamas of this world who love unconditionally. Help me bless others as You have blessed me.
Through Jesus Christ I pray. Amen.

LIFE LESSON #8
Attitude

We cannot control what other people say and do. We can only control what *we* say and what *we* do. Mama Burnley is living proof that we do not have to allow others to direct or dictate our attitude. Mama Burnley's attitude is shaped by love. She has truly accepted the fact that she must love her neighbor as she loves herself. What is your attitude?

Do you give love only to those who love you first? Are you willing to help only those who can repay you? Do you give respect only to those who are in a position to help or hurt you? If the answer to these questions is yes, then it's gut-check time. Even the worst of sinners can be kind to his friends. Prov. 25:21-22 counsels, "If your enemy is hungry, give him food! If he is thirsty, give him something to drink! This will make him feel ashamed of himself, and God will reward you."

There may be someone in your life right now who is a challenge to be around. It could be a neighbor, a co-worker, or a family member. You may have tried everything that you can think of to deal with this person. Nothing seems to work. Have you tried this?

Approach the person and in all sincerity say, "If I have done anything to offend you, I apologize." An attitude of love and concern can break walls of indifference and hostility. Before you can do that, however, you must break down your wall of pride. God does not honor pride. He does honor humility.

Anger and anxiety are normal human emotions. It is natural to reject people who reject us. It is natural to respond angrily when angry darts are thrown our way. As Christians, we are called to do what is unnatural. We are called to pray for our enemies. As human beings, we are powerless to fight the emotions that are dredged up by unkind people. But we can do all things through Christ who strengthens us.

Will we always do it right? Of course not. Mama Burnley would be the first to tell you she is not the woman she used to be. The sweet-natured Mama Burnley of today is the result of years of leaning on the Lord. She is a better person today because of the impact God has had on her life. We are evolving.

The more we practice praying for our enemies, extending the hand of friendship, and being patient even with those who get on our last nerve, the easier it will become.

I heard the great poet and author Maya Angelou deliver a speech at Hampton University. It was just my blessing to find the speech on C-Span as I was cable surfing. Dr. Angelou said we have it within our power to be a healing balm.

Our cheerfulness, courage, kindness, and enthusiasm can be just what the doctor ordered for someone who happens across our path today. We have a choice everyday to either be an H-bomb or an H-balm. We have that choice to make every time we open our mouths.

H-Bomb Versus H-Balm

The words that flow from our lips can either uproot lives like a hydrogen bomb or they can uplift lives like a healing balm. In Matt. 12:34-37 Jesus says,

> For a man's heart determines his speech. A good man's speech reveals the rich treasures within. An evil-hearted man is filled with venom and his speech reveals it. And I tell you this, that you must give an account judgment day for every idle word you speak. Your words now reflect your fate then. Either you will be justified by them or you will be condemned.

James 3:4-6 describes how terribly powerful the tongue is:

> A tiny rudder makes a huge ship turn wherever the pilot wants it to go, even though the winds are strong. So also the tongue is a small thing, but what enormous damage it

can do. A great forest fire can be set on fire by one tiny spark. And the tongue is a flame or fire. It is full of wickedness, and poisons every part of the body. And the tongue is set on fire by hell itself, and can turn our whole lives into a blazing flame of destruction and disaster.

Sticks and stones can break our bones and yes, words can wound and destroy, too. The tongue is a wild creature, that left to its own instincts and inclinations could be as disastrous as a hydrogen bomb in demolishing lives. But it doesn't have to be that way.

We have a powerful ally in taming the tongue—our faith in God. We pray daily to be all that He would have us to be, so that when we open our mouths out will pour a sweet balm and not a bitter dart. The choice is ours. We can be used by the devil to spread hatred and intimidation, or we can be used by God to spread His love and healing.

Jesus said in Matt. 22:37-39, "Love the Lord your God with all your heart and with all your soul and with all your mind. This is the first and greatest commandment. And the second is like it, love your neighbor as yourself."

Let us go forth today on a mission from God to be a healing balm.

Lord,

I yearn to be a healer. Help me to fast every day . . . abstaining from negative thoughts, words, and deeds. Make me a balm.

Through Jesus Christ I pray. Amen.

CHAPTER 9

Out of the Mouths of Babes

THE MOST IMPORTANT LESSONS IN FAITH I have received have come not from ministers but from my own children. I have learned much about God's grace and love from my relationship with Judith, Kelly, and Jeremiah. These children have amazed me with insights beyond their years.

Judith was eight years old when she opened my eyes to my terrible shortcoming, pride. I had gotten home early from work on Christmas Eve, and I was excited about the prospect of baking cookies with Judith and Kelly. Just as we got started, the doorbell rang.

I went to the door and found two men of a different faith who wanted to share their religious beliefs with me. I was annoyed at the interruption but I forced a smile and said I was too busy to talk with them, and I wished them a Merry Christmas. After I shut the door, Judith asked me why I had been so mean to the gentlemen. I told her that I treated them politely. But Judith knew the difference between genuine kindness and polite indifference, and she continued to challenge me. In exasperation, I finally voiced my true opinion. I told her I did not like people making assumptions that I was a sinner that needed saving. After all, those men did not even know me.

Judith listened patiently to my complaint and then responded in words that hit me like a thunderbolt. She said, "Mom, we are all sinners, aren't we?" Those words stopped me in my tracks, and I realized that Judith had cut to the heart of the matter. Yes, we are all sinners, saved by grace.

I hugged Judith and thanked her for helping me to remember that the most important thing about Christmas was not cookies but Christ. He came into the world to save me.

Kelly was born in a veil. Some older people believe that children born encased in a thin membrane have special powers of understanding and prophecy. Kelly has surprised me at times with her spirituality.

Once when she was in preschool I heard her singing a song. She sang, "Listen to Jesus . . . you must listen to Jesus . . . listen to Jesus or He will punish you . . . punish you . . . punish you."

I came running around the corner and asked who had taught her that song. She replied that no one had taught her. I couldn't help feeling that Kelly was some kind of receiver picking up radio signals and transmitting them even though she did not fully understand the meaning. She got my attention.

A few years later Kelly came down with the chicken pox and was unable to play with the other children in the neighborhood. She had to amuse herself alone in the backyard.

Suddenly Willie came running upstairs. "You'll never believe what Kelly is doing," he informed me. He told me that our little kindergartner was in the backyard delivering a sermon to the sky. By the time I got downstairs the sermon was over. But Willie told me what he had overheard.

He said Kelly had spoken vehemently about the need to take care of the children. He said that she had described children that we may pass on the street. She argued that we should not pass these children by, but that we should find out what they need. Again, I felt that Kelly was being used to transmit a message that was beyond her years of comprehension.

Some people say that children play make-believe and that it is nothing we should take seriously. But I respect children because the Bible says God takes children very seriously.

I believe it is very important for Jeremiah to always understand that he is adopted. I don't want him to find out later in life and wonder why we kept that from him. I began to tell him when he was a toddler that he was specially chosen and loved from the very beginning.

Once, when he was two years old, I was telling Jeremiah the story of his adoption. I looked at him and said, "I chose you." Jeremiah interrupted and declared, "No, I chose *you!*" Now that is an awesome thought.

A day or so later I brought up the subject again. I said to Jeremiah, "God chose you...." Before I could complete the sentence Jeremiah responded, "No, God chose *you!*"

My wonderful child Jeremiah spoke a wonderful truth. We are all chosen by God to do great and wonderful things. But we all have a choice to accept or reject God's commission.

My children are all terrific kids, but they are not perfect. They are not angels. But the Bible says that each and every one of these children has a guardian angel. We cannot see these angels, but sometimes I wonder if the children can. We've all seen babies who suddenly break into a smile for no particular reason as they stare into space. Maybe they see something we don't.

As I put Jeremiah to bed one night, he stared at the window and asked, "Do you see him?" I said, "See who? Where?" He pointed and said, "Over there ... by the window...a man ... he can fly... like a butterfly." I asked him to describe the man. "He's a nice man," Jeremiah told me. "He's a policeman. He says Jesus loves me." I asked him if he saw the man often, and he replied that he did.

People may say that this is just a child's overactive imagination, and it could be. But doesn't Jeremiah's strange description fit that of a guardian angel?

Even when my children misbehave, I see lessons of faith. And I wonder how often my children's relationship with me resembles my relationship with God. How many times do I throw a tantrum when things do not work out my way?

And no matter how many times the Lord takes care of my needs, I still scream out in pain and worry. My children will whine, "Mom, I'm hungry . . ." as if I'm not going to feed them.

Or my children will scream when I won't allow them to walk alone to the corner convenience store. I know eventually they will be able to do so, but they do not want to wait. They want everything *now*. And I, too, am guilty of that impatience. But just as my children must yield to me, I too must yield to my Father.

I also have learned that just as I love my children equally, so does our Father. At one time or another each of my children has asked the question, "Who do you love the most?" They are never satisfied with my response that I love them all the same. My two youngest children, Kelly and Jeremiah, often play a cruel game of "She's *my* mommy!" "No, she's *my* mommy!"

I wonder how many of us are guilty of playing the same prideful game. Many of us want to claim some special relationship with our Father. How many of us are guilty of saying, "No, he's *my* Father!"

Regardless of our religion, race, gender, nationality, or sin, we are all His children. He loves us all the same.

The Bible says that to be accepted by God we must have the faith of a child. I witnessed that childlike faith one day when Judith and I were stepping into a swimming pool.

Judith was about three years old and we were vacationing in Florida. Judith didn't know how to swim, so she held my hand as we walked down the steps into the pool. We had walked down a couple of steps when I noticed Judith looking up at me . . . through the water!

I screamed and picked her up quickly, and she was just fine. But I will never forget that look of faith. Judith was in water over her head, yet she never took her eyes off of me. She trusted me to take care of her.

That is the kind of faith we strive for as children of God. Just as Peter was able to walk on water as long as he focused on Jesus, we too can walk through the storms of our lives as long as we keep our eyes on our Father. We hold His hand and we trust Him to bring us safely home.

Please, Father, continue to hold my hand. I am lost without You. I need You. Please, Lord, forgive me for those times I have acted like a spoiled brat. I love You, our Father.

Through Jesus Christ I pray. Amen.

LIFE LESSON #9
Accept God's Amazing Grace

If you ever find yourself wondering whether God is real, just look around you. Who hung the sun in the sky? Who made it possible for you to inhale life-giving air this very moment?

It doesn't take a Phi Beta Kappa to know that only a supreme being could put the planets in orbit and knit an infant's body in a mother's womb.

When we turn our lives over to God, we can be sure that anything that comes our way was either sent by God or allowed by God. God said in Isa. 55:8-9, "This plan of mine is not what you would work out, neither are my thoughts the same as yours! For just as the heavens are higher than the earth, so are my ways higher than yours and my thoughts than yours."

At the beginning of this book, I wrote about an anchorship that I wanted in 1981. I didn't get it. It was another seven years before I was able to land that prized position.

God's timing is not our timing. Just keep putting one foot in front of the other and know that He will work it out. No matter what "it" is.

In the Bible, Jewish history is constantly retold, as a reminder of what God did for the Israelite children. So we too should look back over our history. How many times were you at your wit's end, facing major disappointment, or in the grasp of grief that was so overwhelming you thought you would suffocate? And how many times did God rescue you? He did it before and He will do it again. Trust Him.

A co-worker of mine got that message in a most surprising way. Jimmy Brown, a television photographer, was driving to work before dawn one morning. He was depressed about situations that were beyond his control. As he pondered his problems, a song came on the radio... "Sign ... sign ... everywhere a sign ... "

Jimmy said he looked up, and there in front of him in the bend of the highway was a sign he had never seen before. Someone had plastered a boldly printed poster across a highway sign.

The person who put the sign there could not have known how it would gladden the heart of a weary traveler in life. Jimmy took a picture of the sign to serve as a constant reminder that when the road is dark, look up and ...

Afterword

THERE WERE TIMES when I wondered whether this book would ever be published, but not because of any difficulty in finding a publisher or the words. God laid out everything so perfectly from Don Westbrook's beautiful pictures to my multitalented friend Frank Davis's kind guidance in leading me to a publisher.

However, as the release date for *Going Live* approached, I found myself under more and more pressure. I was attacked by challenges of all kinds.

The Reverend Dr. Charles Stanley wrote in his February 1998 *In Touch* devotional: "Many times a sure sign that you are doing what God has called you to do is opposition. Satan and his workers have one goal in mind, and that is to keep you from being all that God has planned for you to become."

I hope no one gets the impression from reading this book that walking in faith is an easy process. Maybe one day, Lord willing, I will grow into a sweet, elderly lady like Mama Burnley who can sing through the storms of life.

But right now I am like a recovering alcoholic trying to travel the road of righteousness, one day at a time. Sometimes I fall off the wagon and get angry or indulge in a pity party. But through it all I know Jesus saves, which just happens to be the song playing on the radio as I write this.

Jesus often encourages us through fellow believers. That is why I'm so grateful I found a good church family like Bethany United Methodist Church. So often I have been inspired by Rev. Hadley Edwards' stirring sermons, Pastor Larry Faulkner's excellent Sunday school class, and Willie Johnson and Inez

Williams' in-depth Bible study group. If you haven't already, I urge you to find a church home where you can be fed and loved. Eagles soar with eagles. Find spiritual friends who will encourage you in the down times that are inevitable in life.

As I write this concluding word, my friend Pattie is nudging me to look up and behold the glory of God's beautiful rays of sun raining down like spotlights through the clouds. And the contemporary Christian music group Avalon is on the radio singing, "As long as I shall live, I will testify to love. I'll be a witness in the silences when words are not enough. With every breath I take, I will give thanks to God above."

Inspirational author and singer Sheila Walsh said during the 1998 Women of Faith Conference in Baton Rouge that she had a great weight lifted from her when she accepted the fact that *she* is not the Good News. She is only supposed to be a bearer of the Good News.

That is true. We are Christians not Christ. We tell the Good News. *Jesus Christ is the Good News.*

My help comes from the Lord. He speaks to me in quiet reassuring thoughts, reminding me of who He is and who I am. I had one of those sweet conversations when I was feeling low early Thursday morning, December 11, 1997. I do not share this with you lightly. I know there are those who say, "Say what?" when you talk about having a conversation with God. It makes no human sense that there is a God who can and does communicate with us. But we come from a family of faith. Our spirit knows His voice well.

This is what my spirit heard before dawn that December morning. If this message is meant for you, your spirit will know it.

Be still and know that I am God.
I am I am.
I created this world and everything in it.
I gave you life and every other living thing, plant and animal.

Do you really think I cannot help you overcome any obstacle?
I am I am.
I own the cattle on a thousand hills and
my storehouses are filled to overflowing.
I am I am.
What are you afraid of?
If you are afraid of anything but Me, your fear is misplaced.
Fear Me alone.
I am I am.
I give life.
I give peace.
I give joy.
Don't fall for the devil's lies.
He would like you to believe that all is lost.
He wants you to give up, cave in, and pack up.
Tell the devil no and keep putting one foot in front of the other.
That's all I ask.
Walk.
Just walk.
You don't have to run.
Just keep putting one foot in front of the other.
Just keep going.
Persevere to the end.
Finish your course.
Your faithful ancestors are watching and cheering for you from My kingdom.
You cannot believe the rewards
you will find on the other side of the finish line.
There is nothing in this world to compare with the fruits of heaven.
Take all the happiness you have ever known in this life,
multiply it by quadrillion, and you still would not come close to the bliss . . .
The absolute perfect bliss
that awaits My good and faithful servants
on the other side of the finish line.
Study to show yourself approved.
Feast on My Word.
Learn of what I have done for those who have preceded you on earth
and know that anything and everything I have done for them,
I will do for you.

You can have the prosperity and wisdom of Solomon,
the strength and beauty of Esther,
the courage of David and Daniel.
Ask.
The doors of the storehouse are open.
Ask for what you require.
You have not because you ask not.
Trust Me.
Turn all of your cares over to Me.
You are My child.
You are My good and faithful servant in whom I am well pleased.
I made a covenant with your family generations ago to bless you today.
I keep My promises.
Keep yours.
Give as I have given to you.
Love as I have loved you.
Don't give in to Satan's message of doom and gloom.
His days are numbered.
He is a toothless demon who has power if you give it to him
by lending him the use of your mind.
Thoughts are powerful instruments for good or evil.
On whose side are you today?
What are you thinking about?
Are you focusing on Me or circumstances?
Don't fall for Satan's smoke and mirrors.
You are safe and secure from all alarm.
Your fate is already sealed in blood.
Jesus died for your sins.
Jesus prayed for you.
You are Mine.
Focus on that fact and watch your life come into focus.
Watch all those who were troubling you bow before you.
Let My residence within you be seen by all.
Don't hide My light.
Share it.
Trust and obey.

Each One Save One
Vision Statement

We believe that with a mentor,
each child can have the opportunity
to reach his or her fullest potential.
We envision
confident, responsible children,
who are excited about life,
creating safe, caring, productive
families and communities.

If you would like to donate time, money, or any other resource, or if you would just like more information about Each One Save One, please call or write:

Each One Save One
4521 Dryades Steet
New Orleans, LA 70115
(504) 895-3050